Grace or Money

Grace or Money

Rediscovering the Gift of Grace in an Age of Greed

Justin Pack

GREG KOFFORD BOOKS
SALT LAKE CITY

Cover design by Loyd Isao Ericson.

Published in the USA.

ISBN: 978-1-58958-823-3 (paperback)
Also available in ebook.

Greg Kofford Books
P. O. Box 1362
Draper, UT 84020
www.gregkofford.com
facebook.com/gkbooks
twitter.com/gkbooks

Library of Congress Control Number: 2025949785

Contents

Introduction

An 1834 revelation to Joseph Smith declares:

> For the earth is full, and there is enough and to spare; yea, I prepared all things, and have given unto the children of men to be agents unto themselves.
>
> Therefore, if any man shall take of the abundance which I have made, and impart not his portion, according to the law of my gospel, unto the poor and the needy, he shall, with the wicked, lift up his eyes in hell, being in torment. (D&C 104:17–18)

These verses are far more significant than they might appear to the modern reader. For such a reader, there are likely to be two interpretations of this passage. A superficial reading of it might be as follows: (1) "God made a lot of stuff, and He made humans free. We should share with the poor by paying tithing and offerings or we might get in trouble." A less superficial reading might notice the remarkably strong language about people tormented in hell and, in light of this, offer a stronger interpretation along the following lines: (2) "God made more than enough stuff, and He made humans free. God cares deeply about the widow and the orphan and is livid with those who don't seek to help them. We need to do far more to help them."

I think both of these interpretations fall far short of what is truly going on here. The second has the advantage of taking more seriously the plight of the poor but is still far from adequate. Part of the problem is that our *modern* conceptual lenses are shaped by certain ideals and ethical commitments that are very different than *premodern* ideals and ethical commitments. For example, modern economics teaches us that scarcity is basic to the human condition. Contrary to this, though, is the implication of the first line: "For the earth is full, and there is enough and to spare." In other words, scarcity is not natural. Instead, God has "prepared all things" and "there is enough . . . to spare." This does not match what we experience in the modern world, however, and is not how we have been taught to understand our lives. We experience a world where many struggle to get by, both in industrialized countries and in poor countries around the world. We tend to see this as an unfortunate but natural and expected situation given the reality of scarcity.

But, if this verse is rejecting the reality of scarcity and instead asserting that God has created more than enough to go around, why then do we see such poverty? The second verse answers this: because some men "take of the abundance which I have made, and impart not [their] portion, according to the law of my gospel" (v. 18). In other words, there is more than enough for everyone, but some are keeping more than their fair portion, leading to others not getting their share. Scarcity and poverty are not natural; they are the results of human sin—the grotesque failure to care for each other.

To be clear, if you have more than you need and do not share it with "the poor and needy," according to this revelation you will "with the wicked, lift up [your] eyes in hell, being in torment" (v. 18). Stating the issue in these terms is shocking to the modern reader, because we do not tend to see the condition of the "poor and needy" as a reflection of our actions. As a wealthy Christian friend told me, "Are you not the captain of your boat? Is each of us not fiscally responsible for our own lives?" This is something like the standard view of responsibility in modern capitalism. Everyone is responsible for themselves. What you earn is yours, and you can do with it what you will.

In terms of human existence, this is a rather new way of understanding what it is to be human and how we relate to each other (or *don't* relate to each other, as modern hyper-individualism seems to imply). Anthropology has helped us understand that for the majority of human existence, humans saw themselves as intimately connected not only to each other, but also to the plants, animals, spirits, and gods of the world.[1] The world was experienced, very much as the above verses indicate, as full of abundance with more than enough for humans. We could say that human life was marked by an existential abundance—not, as most of us have been erroneously taught about hunter-gatherers, by the struggle to survive.[2] Since this abundance was a gift and not something made by humans, we had to establish and maintain careful relationships with the plants, animals, spirits, and gods that also dwelt in the cosmos—what Marcel Hénaff calls "cosmic civility."[3] The primary threat to the abundance was cosmic incivility. This could take the form of ingratitude, failure to establish or maintain proper relationships with non-human peoples, or, perhaps worst of all, hoarding the abundance for oneself at the expense of others.

Robert Bellah points out that some of humankind's closest relatives, chimpanzees and gorillas, are led by alpha males that dominate everyone

1. Marshall Sahlins, *The New Science of the Enchanted Universe: An Anthropology of Most of Humanity*.

2. Marshall Sahlins, *Stone Age Economics*.

3. Marcel Hénaff, *The Price of Truth: Gift, Money and Philosophy*.

else and monopolize females. He argues that for hundreds of thousands of years—most of our existence—humans worked together to turn the tables and dominate the wannabe alpha males.[4] Doing so helped to establish and maintain the relative equality that has been the norm of most human communities until the Neolithic Revolution.[5] This promoted not only the relative equality and freedom of humankind,[6] but it also prevented the breaking of cosmic civility. The abundance of the cosmos can only be preserved if we stop those who would hoard it for themselves and fail to act appropriately with the non-human world.

If we go back and read the verses that opened this introduction in light of this brief account of cosmic civility, we can see God declaring that the abundance He has prepared gives humans the freedom to choose how to act. Furthermore, He expresses His intense anger with those who would ruin abundance by keeping for themselves what is meant for all of us.

Let me make what I am arguing starker. Heaven is abundant. When God says that "the earth is full, and there is enough and to spare; yea, I prepared all things," He is declaring that just as humankind was created in the image of God, the earth was created in the image of heaven. The abundance of heaven and the earth is free—it is a gift. I will call this abundance the "order of grace." Grace is not just the gift of salvation through Jesus Christ. Grace is the logic of heaven.

Thus, to "take of the abundance which I have made, and impart not his portion, according to the law of my gospel, unto the poor and the needy" is not merely to harm God's children that He loves; it is to reject the order of grace by rejecting the abundance of heaven on Earth. It is to replace the order of grace with the order of merit, or, to state the point another way, to replace grace with money.

Because modernity has disenchanted the cosmos, we live in grace-less times. We struggle to understand the order of grace because of the ubiquity of money. By money, I don't just mean cash and coins, I mean a counterorder to grace. Grace is unreflexive; money is calculative. Grace is qualitative; money is quantitative. Grace is given; money is exchanged. In many ways, grace and money are opposite orders, and we must choose one or the other.

---

4. Robert N. Bellah, *Religion in Human Evolution: From the Paleolithic to the Axial Age.*

5. James Suzman, *Affluence Without Abundance: What We Can Learn from the World's Most Successful Civilisation*; David Graeber and David Wengrow, *The Dawn of Everything: A New History of Humanity.*

6. Graeber and Wengrow.

If this is correct, then there is no money in heaven. On the one hand, there would be no need for it. But on the other, it *must* be so because money is dangerous. In the New Testament, the first epistle to Timothy famously and aggressively claims "the love of money is the root of all evil" (1 Tim. 6:10). This is one of the most well-known and quoted verses in the New Testament. In my experience, however, it is almost always followed up with the assured clarification that it is the *love* of money and not money itself that is the problem.

This is really a strange reaction when you think about it. Imagine if the Bible said that "the love of heroin is the root of all evil," and the consistent response was to clarify that it is the *love* of heroin and not heroin itself that is the problem. I mean, sure, I guess it is the *love* of heroin that is the problem for heroin addicts, but this seems like a technicality because heroin is seen as obviously dangerous.

This emphasis on the *love* of money over money itself implies that money is not like heroin. Indeed, money is now often treated as a neutral tool that can be used for many things. Can it be abused? Yes. But that isn't the fault of money, we are told. It is the fault of people who abuse it.

But if this translation is correct, it seems like it would be a terrible mistake to try and weaken Paul's claim here. He doesn't say that the love of money causes some minor problems. He says it is "the root of all evil." This translation from the King James Bible seems to present the love of money as not just a highly dangerous sin, but *the* keystone sin: all evil comes from it. This is an astonishing claim when stated this way. It seems to imply that if we want to get rid of evil, or at least as much of it as possible, we should start with the love of money. When stated this way, it sure sounds like money—or the love of money—is something far worse than heroin.

Now, some might be quick to point out that other translations are slightly different. Both the NIV and the ESV translate this verse as "For the love of money is a root of all kinds of evils." This does not present the love of money as a keystone sin; instead it is portrayed like a Pandora's Box. Maybe it is not the root of *all* sin, but it unleashes "all kinds of evils." Again, much worse than heroin.

In light of the gravity of the danger here, why is there such a rush to point out that it is the *love* of money and not money itself that is the problem? The same epistle to Timothy even calls money "filthy lucre" (1 Tim. 3:3, 8). Why the knee-jerk desire to exculpate "filthy lucre"? Shouldn't we be avoiding it like the plague? Why do we protest so much when the meaning seems clear?

This justificatory reaction is all the more surprising when compared with ancient ideas about money. The claim that money is a neutral tool would have been seen as laughably ridiculous in the ancient world. If anything, it was clear to them that money is terribly addicting—not unlike heroin—and, as such, it is extremely dangerous. The Greek philosopher Socrates accused the people of Athens of being obsessed with money, fame, and power to the detriment of their souls. His protégé, Plato, banned merchants from the ideal city he describes in *The Republic* and attacked the Sophists for selling wisdom for money. Aristotle condemned *pleonexia* (greed for wealth) as something that could undermine community and democracy.

For these and many other ancient thinkers, the problem was not just how addictive money could be. Aristotle claimed money is supremely weird or "unnatural" because it can give birth to itself.[7] He means by this that money is highly protean and can do very strange things.

The unnaturalness or weirdness of money is all around us now. A friend related to me with wonder that their home, which they bought ten years ago for $100,000, is now worth $400,000. They have done nothing to increase its value. It has given birth to itself—fourfold what they bought it for. There is no shortage of methods for trying to take advantage of these strange plastic powers of money: myriad schemes to develop "passive income" (make money without working) or Dave Ramsey–inspired plans to invest $100 each month and retire when these investments have grown into a million dollars. On the other side, a sharp rise in inflation can mercilessly wipe out someone's life savings. The poor decisions of a few can crash stock prices for everyone. Cryptocurrencies swing wildly, attracting speculators and worrying regulators. A new cryptocurrency strategically names itself "stablecoin." Money can do very strange, unpredictable things.

Once money becomes widespread in a society, it can threaten the stability of everything. Ancient and medieval societies were often at the mercy of the volatility of money—so much so that in medieval Europe, efforts were made by rulers to fix prices on basic foodstuffs lest the unpredictably shifting prices lead to revolution. As historian Joel Kaye notes, "the most common theme in the medieval attitude toward money was its role as a solvent. It was seen as a disturbing and distorting element, an overturner

7. Aristotle, *Politics*, book I, chapters 8–11.

of social order, an instrument of chaos."[8] It is interesting to note that on this account money is not just ethically dangerous but ontologically destabilizing to reality itself. As Karl Marx famously put it, "All that is solid melts into air," or, as Roman Stoic Seneca writes, "[w]e ask not what a thing is but what it costs."[9]

Worse, humans that embrace the logic of money risk becoming like it—that is to say, by ancient moral standards, they become protean, weird, and inhuman. This was why merchants were so despised by many Axial thinkers.[10] Just as money doesn't care about humans, merchants seeking to make money have a reputation for taking advantage of others in order to profit. They may act like they care, but it is just a show to either keep a customer or trick a buyer. The merchant changes shape to manipulate a situation to their advantage. This not only involves tricking others like a merchant, but, like a contemporary student or an employee, submitting themselves to absurd demands in inhuman systems that require acting in bizarre ways. The word most commonly used to describe the nonsensical tasks required in inhuman money-making systems is "bullshit."

Let me pause here for my Latter-day Saint readers who, like myself, were taught not to swear. My father used to say, "A dirty mouth is a sign of an empty mind." My mother got so upset when a scene in *Karate Kid* had three swear words in a span of ten seconds that she turned it off and took it right back to the rental store. Despite this, "bullshit" or "BS" will be a topic of two entire chapters in this book. Why not avoid the term or the topic? Because I think BS is one of the greatest dangers of our time and a soul-destroying threat to our children. We need to be clear about it and face it head on. Turning away from it or shuffling it to the side with euphemisms will not do. It is not used here as a vulgar term, but as a vulgar phenomenon we need to address.

"Bullshit" turns out to be a remarkably rich word of surprisingly philosophical import.[11] It can describe tasks that we find pointless but must do in order to pass a class or earn a grade; it can describe a variety of actions in which we try to look like we know something when we don't or like we are busy working when we are not; it can describe being fake or lying

---

8. Joel Kaye, *Economy and Nature in the Fourteenth Century: Money, Market Exchange and the Emergence of Scientific Thought*, 39; Jacques Le Goff, *Money and the Middle Ages: An Essay in Historical Anthropology*.

9. Lucius Annaeus Seneca, *Letters on Ethics: To Lucilius*, 115.10.

10. Hénaff, *The Price of Truth*.

11. Harry G. Frankfurt, *On Bullshit*.

to get ahead; it can describe the weirdness necessitated by a money-driven society. A world of money will tend to be a world of BS.

In a world of money, many become accustomed to BS. It is normalized, even while being commonly lambasted. There are many films, novels, and philosophical treatises condemning the alienation, exploitation, and absurdity of this modern condition. And yet, despite these contemporary criticisms—which, we should add, occur in addition to all the ancient and premodern criticisms about money and merchants—many seem convinced that there is no alternative or that this is best we can hope for.

There are two stories to be told here. One concerns how the world of money became ascendant in modernity. This involves the question of what kinds of arguments or events could overthrow traditional moral suspicions of money, markets, and merchants.[12] The second concerns why, despite powerful criticisms, money maintains such a hold on our moral imaginary. The answer I will offer to this second question is meritocracy.

There are different versions of meritocracy, including some in antiquity. For our purposes here, I mean the idea that hard work and ingenuity should be rewarded—that those who perform the best and work the hardest should be put into positions of power and influence. This is often reduced to the claim that hard work leads to success. As I have argued in *Meritocracy Mingled with Scripture*, the ideals of meritocracy have become deeply intertwined with self-identity, modern social order, and religion for many Americans.[13] More specifically, the logic of merit increasingly functions as a religion, replacing the order of grace in the religions it infiltrates. Meritocracy takes the inequalities and poverty all around us and turns it into a supposedly just order: the poor deserve their place for not working, the rich deserve their place for working. Everything is in its right place. In terms of Christianity, the justice promised in the next life is already here! God's future justice is traded for meritocracy's current supposed justice.

This book is a combination of two projects I've been intending to write. The first was going to be a panegyric on grace. Grace has been a concern of various twentieth-century French philosophers, but I became particularly fascinated with it while reading anthropology texts and Indigenous authors. These authors helped me see that the typical Christian understanding of grace that associates it with salvation is too narrow. Grace is an entire order with its own particular logic. The logic of grace is not entirely

12. Justin Pack, *Money and Thoughtlessness: A Genealogy and Defense of the Traditional Suspicions of Money and Merchants.*

13. Justin Pack, *Meritocracy Mingled with Scripture.*

lost today, and, indeed, some authors have shown that it is omnipresent even in modern society—albeit in small, often unrecognized ways.[14] The more I learned about non-Western cultures and traditions, the more I saw the logic of grace in scripture. The more I saw grace, the more I wondered why it is so hard for many to see.

The second book I intended to write was a polemic to be entitled *Money and Bullshit*. My primary philosophical concerns center on thoughtlessness, and I have already written a book entitled *Money and Thoughtlessness*. After writing that book, I realized that it was not enough to argue that money causes a certain kind of dangerous thoughtlessness—a claim I still agree with. The more I wrote and thought about money, the more I became struck by how utterly weird it is and how it leads people seeking it to do weird things—stupid things they don't want to do, but end up doing anyways because of the desire for money. Worse, since money has become so ubiquitous, its weirdness is infusing our institutions, creating a warped and spiritually stunted society. My favorite philosopher, Hannah Arendt, had already drawn my attention to the ways that people will warp and twist themselves into terrible shapes to accomplish certain goals. I was struck by how much her descriptions of Rahel Varnhagen and Adolf Eichmann reminded me of the "BS" students and jobholders tolerate and perform. As an undergraduate and graduate student, I remember students constantly talking about "BS-ing on the test," "taking some BS class," "BS assignments," "BS readings," and so on. Jobs are full of this sort of thing too.

No topic gets my undergraduate students more riled up than BS. Their lives are full of it: BS they have to put up with, BS they themselves are doing, BS they will have to do. It is everywhere. They hate it. Yet they believe there is no alternative.

When housing prices skyrocketed during and after the COVID-19 pandemic and I found myself, like many millennials, locked out of home ownership, I was struck not only by how fast one gets left behind when one cannot afford a house, but how much all forms of becoming wealthy involve taking advantage of the weirdness of money and markets. Contrary to the common idea that wealth is the result of hard work, wealth is most often the result of breaking the proportionality of work and financial gain. In other words, wealth comes when you start to make far more money than what you work for. Having your home quadruple in value while doing nothing is a good example of this. But, so is getting rich off financial

---

14. Jacques T. Godbout and Alain Caillé, *The World of the Gift*.

speculation, investments, a hit song, a viral video, a popular app, and so on. *All wealth is the result of some sort of luck or disproportionate BS.*

I've long thought of BS-ing as related to disingenuity, and both as opposites of integrity. The problem with a world of money is not just that it leads to thoughtlessness, but that it leads to a world of BS. It rewards those who are willing to compromise their integrity and BS. Much of our education system is designed to inculcate not just obedience, but ideally proactive BS-ing.

As I approached these projects, it became apparent that these issues are two sides of the same coin. When thinking and writing about the order of grace, I had to work against the currently normalized assumptions of *homo economicus*. On the other side, to estrange these assumptions, I needed to contrast the world of money with the grace-full form of existence that we can find in anthropology, Indigenous writing, Christian scripture, and other sources. In light of their either/or relationship, this book is a combination of a panegyric on grace and a polemic against money.

Before outlining the structure of this book, let me address one more issue. Specifically, why am I publishing this with a Mormon studies press? There are two reasons: first, I was raised Latter-day Saint and experienced intense (and philosophically interesting) contradictions between grace and money that I want to explore. For example, when I was a missionary, my particular mission, like many other missions at the time (but not all), leaned heavily into quantified systems of management and incentivization. Every day we had to track whether we got up on time, left the house by a certain time, got home on time, and went to sleep on time—and we had to report this weekly to the higher-ups. Compliance with these targets was considered indicative of our faith and obedience. We also kept track of all our daily activities. Sometimes there were rewards for high performance. Even when there were not specific incentives or rewards, these numbers were often shared with the other missionaries in our area and thus helped to establish our esteem in the eyes of others (and often ourselves). The better and more faithful you were, the higher your numbers should be.

This structure, of course, led to all sorts of BS-ing. Many missionaries worked with an eye on their stats instead of their ostensive task of helping bring people to Christ. We were often taught which kind of methods could help bring about the best results. There was a strong focus on efficiency. This created an interesting tension, as some missionaries who didn't buy into this number-focused incentive system quietly went about their business trying to be good missionaries without paying much attention to the number games. Those perceived to be overly obsessed with numbers were hilariously labeled "Pharisees."

After my mission, church-wide changes were made to move away from the business model of management I'd experienced. I bring this example up to point out the tension between the Mormon ethic and the spirit of capitalism, and the order of grace which is not only pervasive in the Bible but also in Latter-day Saint scripture like The Book of Mormon and the Doctrine and Covenants. Mormonism is a particularly good place to explore these tensions.

The second reason for turning to a Mormon studies press is that it allows me to use the full force of scriptural injunctions for grace and against money. I can argue for the existence of the order of grace through anthropology and Indigenous writing—indeed, this is what I will be doing in the first chapter—but this may end up being an abstract exercise for some readers. There is something far more powerful in the claim that the order of grace is omnipresent in the scriptures of a living tradition but shockingly obscured by problematic commitments to meritocracy. This is a version of one of the great questions that has preoccupied sociologists, philosophers, and historians: how Christians, so traditionally critical of money, embraced capitalism.

I am not aiming only at a Latter-day Saint audience, however. These questions are, I think, philosophically important for Christians and non-Christians alike. But writing to a Mormon audience will allow me to heighten the tension of this problem by treating it as a live, critical problem, instead of an abstract one. There is a risk of alienating non-Mormon or nonreligious readers as a result, but it is my contention that these issues are just as relevant to them.

Let me outline how I will proceed.

In Chapter 1, I will introduce the basic reality of abundance as evidenced in anthropology and Indigenous writing. In the last fifty years, there has been a radical change in thinking about the Neolithic Revolution (also known as the agricultural revolution). While it is common now to think of hunter-gatherers as miserable, constantly starved, primitive peoples, anthropology is revealing almost the opposite is true. Hunter-gatherers lived in abundance in more ways than one. As I have already indicated in this introduction, there was more than enough food. The question, then, is what happened to the experience of abundance? We will see that the anthropological evidence indicates that the loss of abundance comes with the Neolithic Revolution.

In Chapter 2, I will attempt to define the order of grace by building on the anthropological evidence presented in the first chapter, especially by looking into the logic of gift cultures and supplementing it with Latter-day Saint scripture. Verses like those that I used to open this introduction are ubiquitous throughout the scriptures. I will elaborate my claim that heaven is grace-full and that the earth is created in the image of heaven. I will also further elaborate how the scriptures describe the fall from grace.

In Chapter 3, I will turn to the foil of the order of grace and the order of money. Specifically, this chapter will attempt to estrange us from the current normalization of money by showing how weird it is. To do so I will look at the criticisms of money from ancient philosophers like Plato and Aristotle, and also examine how some modern philosophers, like John Locke and Johann Gottlieb Fichte, tried to deal with the weirdness of money. We will then look at some contemporary practices that have now become normalized but, when looked through the lens of premodern thinkers, appear irrational and unethical.

In order to help problematize the modern filter or the modern way of seeing and understanding these issues, I will turn to the ideology of meritocracy in Chapter 4. While I have dealt with this in *Meritocracy Mingled with Scripture*, it will be helpful to revisit these issues in order to see how meritocracy shapes our sense of identity in capitalism and how it functions as a kind of religion.

This book will explore the ways money is related not only to thoughtlessness, but also to the ubiquity of BS-ing in modern life. A world of money will tend to be a world of BS. In Chapter 5 I will elaborate on this by turning to the philosophy of Hannah Arendt. While the philosopher Harry Frankfurt and the anthropologist David Graeber have also offered compelling accounts of BS, I will argue that Arendt's account is particularly helpful.

With the concept of BS defined, Chapter 6 will examine how the world of money becomes a world of BS. This is a problem for all of us, although I will delve into the specifics of two institutions in which I have spent much of my life: Christianity (specifically Mormonism) and academia. I am particularly interested in how money and BS-ing undermines the integrity of those living in the modern world, creating a spiritually and ethically stunted disingenuity.

Lastly, in the conclusion I will discuss how the recovery of the order of grace can help wake us up and heal us from the world of money and BS.

1. Abundance

God is abundance. Heaven is abundance. Neither of these claims is controversial, and the scriptures are full of declarations of this abundance and invitations to participate in it:

> Ho, every one that thirsteth, come ye to the waters, and he that hath no money; come ye, buy, and eat; yea, come, buy wine and milk without money and without price. (Isa. 55:1)
>
> The thief cometh not, but for to steal, and to kill, and to destroy: I am come that they might have life, and that they might have *it* more abundantly. (John 10:10)
>
> Yea, I know that God will give liberally to him that asketh. (2 Ne. 4:35)

I am going to make an argument about what this abundance means and implies, because I think we often gravely misunderstand it. Abundance is not merely a Heavenly Father with many material and spiritual gifts that He wants to give us; it is rather an order or a logic, a way of life—a way of understanding the world and relating to each other. To understand and live abundance is to live a very different way than we do now.

To clarify what I mean, let's begin with two kinds of narratives we tell ourselves about abundance.

1. The biblical origin story begins with abundance. Adam and Eve are placed in the Garden of Eden, an earthly paradise full of beautiful trees that provide all sorts of good food. But, after eating the fruit of the tree of knowledge of good and evil, they find themselves expelled out of the garden and into the world, which is often in scripture described as a wilderness. Eve is cursed to have painful childbirth, to desire her husband, and to be ruled by him (Gen. 3:16). Adam is cursed with the loss of abundance and the necessity to work hard to get food, and to eventually die (Gen. 3:17–19). They enter the realm of scarcity.

Thus, the biblical origin story can be read as a loss of abundance and its replacement with scarcity. But, it is also a story of the promise of a return to abundance, the repeated promise of "a land flowing with milk and honey" (Ex. 3:17). This promise is not for an exit from the world; it is a promise for a place within this world that is abundant. While it may not mean doing no work at all, it means lots of help from the bees and the domesticated animals. The promised land is a repeated promise of abundance we see from God for His peoples: Israel, Lehi, the pioneers, and so on.

Structurally, this narrative places human existence between two abundances: an abundance at the beginning, which we have lost; and an abundance in the future that awaits us (whether a promised land or the entrance into heaven in the next life). The space between is one of scarcity and difficulty. Even when a promised land is found, it is often later lost or compromised. Having fallen into the wilderness of scarcity, we aim to ascend up the other side to abundance.

Oddly, there is sometimes a weird and frustrating association of the United States with *the* or *a* promised land. Despite an original intense antipathy to the United States after the killing of Joseph Smith and the driving out of Mormons from the States into Mexico, after the turn of the century, The Church of Jesus Christ of Latter-day Saints and its culture embraced the United States, often invoking it as a special promised land and creating a divinization of America as a promised land.[1] Thus, at times Latter-day Saints will use problematic, laudatory language that treats the United States like a promised land of abundance. But, I would claim, this functions against the larger backdrop of our current existence being in the valley of scarcity and, despite the supposed blessing of living in the United States, it is tacitly recognized that there are still many problems and that genuine abundance will have to wait for the next life or some future state.

2. With regard to abundance, the secular narrative of human progress is structurally quite similar. The typical story we moderns tell ourselves about human progress runs something like this: the first humans were hunter-gatherers; they lived a miserable, impoverished existence, perpetually scrounging around for anything to eat; then, agriculture was discovered and this resulted in the first leap forward for humankind. We could settle down, relying on regular and more predictable patterns of food production. We could specialize, and this resulted, in time, for art and the development of culture. The first great civilizations in Egypt, Mesopotamia, China, and India were created thanks to agriculture.

The next stage in human progress was the classical age, also known as the axial age (roughly 800 to 200 BCE) because of how pivotal it was to human history. This was the time of ancient Greece, Rome, China, and India. Many of the world's religious, philosophical, and artistic traditions appear in this period: Judaism, Hinduism, Buddhism, Daoism, Confucianism, Zoroastrianism, Greek and Roman philosophy, Socrates, Plato, Aristotle, beautiful statues, wonderful buildings, towering empires—what a time!

Sadly, in the West at least (the story goes), there was a major bump in the road with the fall of Rome and the ensuing Dark Ages, but eventually,

1. Kathleen Flake, *The Politics of American Religious Identity: The Seating of Senator Reed Smoot, Mormon Apostle.*

in the medieval era and especially with the Renaissance, things started to turn around and get back on track. However, they really took off with the rise of modern science and the resulting modern technologies. Modernity, then, was the next and greatest leap forward for humankind, as science and the Enlightenment helped us to make great discoveries and develop all sorts of new knowledge. We have much to be grateful for: modern medicine, modern communication, the modern economy—life has never been better. No, it isn't perfect. There are still problems. But it is better than ever and we have much to look forward to!

We learn some variation of this narrative of progress early on. When my son was in first grade, his class was working hard to prepare a play about California. One day, he turned to me and said: "Dad, aren't you happy to live in the greatest country in the history of the world?" He had barely started learning how to do subtraction, but he was already being inundated with stories of patriotism and progress.

It is worth noting the ideological function of narratives of progress. They help us feel good about ourselves and about the present. They give us hope for the future. They function like a theodicy (an explanation for why an all-powerful and loving God allows evils to exist). Again, yes, there are problems with modern life, but we are so blessed! Life is better than ever before, and it will get ever better. We want to believe this. It makes us feel special. For many, it makes us feel powerful and competent. We have done this! We are part of a project to improve the human condition and have worked together to make it happen. Rejoice!

In the secular narrative of progress, there is no fall from abundance into scarcity; there is instead an ongoing ascent out of scarcity. Due to this parallel, the secular and Christian narratives can be combined, often with insidious effects, to frame the economy or the modern nation as divine, creating odd and idolatrous patriotisms and faiths (in technology or neoliberalism for example). Notice that in the narrative of progress, abundance is located temporally both here in the present but also forthcoming in the future. Compared to the earlier peoples and civilizations, we are told we have a far greater abundance than they ever accomplished. But, thanks to our ingenuity and technology, the future should be even better. For some Christians, the claimed abundance of modern life is an indication that we are blessed by God, and, sometimes by extension, that these blessings are a result of our moral goodness. This is an example of the toxic mixture of narratives that can emerge: the ostensible abundance of my country means my country (and my people) are, overall, righteous. God = country = progress = pride = moral goodness.

One of the odd effects of this dual temporality of abundance (both in the present but also in the future) is that it enables defenders of the status quo to invoke the present or future abundance as needed. The present abundance is often used as evidence of our moral goodness and for rejecting the need for any radical changes. But, when faced with trenchant criticism of the status quo (too much inequality, homelessness, drug addiction, exploitation, alienation, environmental crisis, and so on), the future abundance is often invoked in combination with the supposed lack of abundance in the past: "Yes, there are problems, but what we have is still better than things used to be and doing things the way we are is the best guarantee that we will alleviate these problems in the future!"

Considering the empowering and comforting effects of narratives of progress, it is unsurprising that many are often deeply invested in these narratives.[2] Furthermore, it is also not surprising that when evidence that these narratives are critically flawed arises, it tends to be dismissed or ignored because it is threatening not only to our sense of meaning but also to our identity and sense of moral goodness. Arguably, this is what has happened with the overwhelming evidence about the current environmental crisis: it seems our "progress" is self-undermining and we are destroying our own world. This should cause us to pause, but it seems we have too much tied up in these delusions to stop and think about what we are doing. Denial is easier than facing up to the implications of the environmental crisis.

Critically, in the last fifty years there has been a revolution in anthropology that reveals a completely different picture of the history of abundance. It has crucial, and often unpleasant, implications for how we understand the meaning of abundance and modern identity. Not surprisingly, many have been slow to accept or recognize what this means for our modern narratives. Let's turn to this reversal and see what exactly is happening here.

The Original Affluent Society

About fifty years ago, Marshall Sahlins published "The Original Affluent Society," an essay that later became the first chapter in his *Stone Age Economics*. While not without problems, it was the opening salvo of the fundamental reorientation that followed, not just because of its radical implications, but also because Sahlins was direct and provocative in his argument.

Sahlins begins by noting some perplexing behavior of the San people of Namibia (problematically more commonly known as the "bushmen" of

2. Justin Pack, *Meritocracy Mingled with Scripture.*

the Kalahari). First, when offered food, they tended to just gobble it down without saving any for the future.[3] In light of the modern stereotype that hunter-gatherers are constantly and desperately seeking food, this seemed to evidence a lack of foresight, an inability to plan for the future. Second, when offered clothing, they would often try it on, seem quite happy to have it, only for it to be found discarded later. What is going on here?

The key to understanding this "prodigality" is to understand that hunter-gatherers experience themselves as living in abundance. There is no need to save food, because there is plenty of food. You just have to know where to find it and be willing to move around to get it. Much of this depends on the seasons; at certain times of year there may be a glut of acorns, the salmon run multiple times throughout the year, tubers are available in the winter, and so forth. As long as you have the kind of intimate knowledge of flora and fauna that hunter-gatherers have, there is plenty. It is not surprising, then, that when offered food, they gladly eat it up without bothering to save some for later. There is no need. Furthermore, when offered clothing, they find it interesting but ultimately don't want to carry around more than they need because of the necessity to move around.

The first thing to note is that anthropologists had often completely misread the hunter-gatherer experience. Sahlins says that this was sometimes because of disruptions of the ecosystems they lived in. As modern civilizations encroached, natural environments were altered and impoverished. Additionally, hunter-gatherers were often forced out of their traditional territories into some of the least desirable places. As a result, many suffered and were forced to abandon their traditional ways of life. What some anthropologists mistook as the impoverished way of life of hunter-gatherers was actually a reflection of disruption caused by modern colonialism. Furthermore, and rather pathetically, Sahlins also claims that some anthropologists mistook "exotic" practices, like eating bugs, for desperation. After all, civilized people eat cows, not bugs.

But, when anthropologists carefully tracked the daily activity of the San, they discovered something amazing:

> A good case can be made that hunters and gatherers work less than we do; and, rather than a continuous travail, the food quest is intermittent, leisure abundant, and there is a greater amount of sleep in the daytime per capita per year than in and other condition of society.[4]

3. Marshall Sahlins *Stone Age Economics.*
4. Sahlins, 14.

They were getting more than enough nutrition while working less than what we do to obtain it. This meant that they had more free time than we do.

We are taught in modern life to value having money and being able to buy things. We spend much of our time seeking to accumulate stuff that we think will make us happy. As such, when we look at "primitive" people with very few things, we tend to assume it must be a miserable kind of existence. But Sahlins calls hunter-gatherers the "Original Affluent Society." They don't experience their life as impoverished:

> The world's most primitive people have few possessions, but they are not poor. Poverty is not a certain small amount of goods, nor is it just a relation between means and ends; above all it is a relation between people. Poverty is a social status. As such it is the invention of civilization.[5]

To be clear: the claim here is a reversal of our modern ideas about scarcity and abundance. Hunter-gatherers do not experience themselves as constantly dealing with scarcity. They experience themselves as living in abundance. Ironically, it is instead those that live in civilizations that experience the most scarcity. Here Sahlins drives the point home:

> Above all, what about the world today? One-third to one-half of humanity are said to go to bed hungry every night. In the Old Stone Age the fraction must have been much smaller. *This* is the era of hunger unprecedented. Now, in the time of the greatest technical power, is starvation an institution. Reverse another venerable formula: the amount of hunger increases relatively and absolutely with the evolution of culture.[6]

Clearly Sahlins is being provocative here, but his point is a powerful one. He claims hunter-gatherers live in a kind of "Zen affluence" where they have fewer desires and needs for stuff, and so they are happier with less. Meanwhile, we are so pumped full of advertisements and consumer promises that despite our modern abundance, most of us end up with an intense feeling of lack—we don't have a nice enough car, a big enough house (if we can afford a house at all), or that dream vacation. We live in what I would call "existential scarcity," as opposed to the "existential affluence" of hunter-gatherer life. Sadly, for all our "superiority" and freedoms, we are often not happy: "it was not until culture neared the height of its material achievements that it erected a shrine to the Unattainable: *Infinite Needs.*"[7]

---

5. Sahlins, 37.
6. Sahlins, 36.
7. Sahlins, 39.

The Neolithic Revolution

What if Sahlins is correct? What implications follow from his claims?

According to the narrative of progress, hunter-gatherers are the most "primitive" kind of human beings. Supposedly, the first leap forward in the human condition occurred with the neolithic revolution and the discovery of agriculture. This allowed, the story goes, for the development of cities and early civilizations. Here we begin to see the construction of great temples, impressive sculptures, art, new technologies, empires, and so on. Surely this was an advance over the miserable life of hunter-gatherers.

Except, if Sahlins is correct, something is now off about this story. If hunter-gatherers lived in abundance, why would they begin to farm? Farming is difficult and involves a lot of drudgery, such as bending over pulling weeds in the hot sun. Some anthropologists have suggested that hunter-gatherers didn't jump into lifelong farming but rather dabbled with it as an experiment or a small side project at first. James C. Scott suggests that they might have thrown seeds into the wet banks of streambeds knowing that they would not have to remain watering or tending these seeds.[8] If they grew, great. If they didn't, it was no loss. David Graeber and David Wengrow suggest farming might have been playful or ritualized at first, and that instead of a clearly superior method that was immediately and widely embraced, it "hopped, stumbled and bluffed its way around the world."[9]

Contrary to crude stereotypes, hunter-gatherers were not stupid. For example, Sahlins points out that the Hadza, the neighbors of the San, "reject the neolithic revolution in order to *keep* their leisure."[10] They see the drudgery of agriculture and reject it.

The key to agriculture is making someone else do the work. This is why Scott says the current scholarly consensus is that agriculture began at gunpoint—people didn't start doing it because it was better; they did so because they were forced to by others.[11] This shouldn't come as a surprise to readers of the Bible, which is narratively anchored in the enslavement of Israel in Egypt and the palpable anger against the "whore of Babylon." But biblical anger is not just directed against agricultural empires; it is also

8. James C. Scott, *Against the Grain: A Deep History of the Earliest States*, 66.

9. David Graeber and David Wengrow, *The Dawn of Everything: A New History of Humanity*, 249.

10. Marshall Sahlins, *Stone Age Economics*, 14.

11. Scott, *Against the Grain.*

aimed at those within Israel who would take advantage of others. Take for example Nehemiah 5:3–7:

> We have mortgaged our lands, vineyards, and houses, that we might buy corn, because of the dearth.
>
> There were also that said, We have borrowed money for the king's tribute, and that upon our lands and vineyards.
>
> Yet now our flesh is as the flesh of our brethren, our children as their children: and, lo, we bring into bondage our sons and our daughters to be servants, and some of our daughters are brought unto bondage already: neither is it in our power to redeem them; for other men have our lands and vineyards.
>
> And I was very angry when I heard their cry and these words.
>
> Then I consulted with myself, and I rebuked the nobles, and the rulers, and said unto them, Ye exact usury, every one of his brother. And I set a great assembly against them.

What we see in this passage is the problem of predatory lending. The wealthy have offered loans to the poor (almost always with exorbitant interest rates) with the malicious intent of forcing them into servitude if and when they cannot pay these loans back. This practice was widespread in the ancient world and led to cycles of debt forgiveness through debt jubilees.[12] Unlike raiding another community to capture and enslave them as laborers and servants, which was bad enough when done by Egypt or the Assyrians to Israel, this method works internally with the wealthy forcing the poor into servitude. It is, as these verses indicate, taking advantage of your own brother. The tone of this and similar moments, especially in the Old Testament, borders on exasperation and incredulity. If you don't like being sold into bondage, don't do it to your own brother!

This is the way the post-neolithic world was. Because of the misery of agricultural work, agricultural civilizations were based on the exploitation of laborers and servants and became machines for accumulating people internally and externally:

> The entire exercise in early state formation is one of standardization and abstraction required to deal with units of labor, grain, land and rations. Essential to the standardization is the very invention of a standard nomenclature, through writing, of all the essential categories—receipts, work orders, labors, dues, and so on. The creation and imposition of written code throughout the city-state replaced vernacular judgements and was itself a distance-demolishing technology that held sway throughout the small realm. Labor standards were developed for such tasks as ploughing, harrowing, or sowing.

---

12. Michael Hudson, *...And Forgive Them Their Debts: Lending, Foreclosure and Redemption from Bronze Age Finance to the Jubilee Year.*

> Something like 'work points' were created, showing credits and debits in work assignments. Standards of classification and quality were specified for fish, oil, and textiles—which were differentiated by weight and mesh. Livestock, slaves and laborers were classified by gender and age. In embryonic form, the vital statistic of an appropriating state aiming to extract as much value as possible from its land and people is already in evidence.[13]

Not surprisingly, people often tried to escape the cities into the hills.[14] The Bible is written by one such group that created a semi-nomadic, heroic warrior culture that defined itself over and against these cities while still borrowing some practices from them like patriarchy, hierarchy, and the domestication of animals.[15]

We are only scratching the surface here. The Neolithic Revolution unleashed a whole host of evils upon the world: inequality, hierarchy, patriarchy, famine, epidemics, wars, empires, and so on.[16] Is it any wonder that hunter-gatherers avoided agriculture?

Of course, to cover up the immense suffering these early civilizations caused and convince themselves that they were not so bad, they created intense propaganda that both denigrated those outside of "civilization" and deified themselves. The very language of "civilized" vs. "primitive" reflects these goals, and even today we continue to be taken in by this kind of propaganda:

> Historical humankind has been mesmerized by the narrative of progress and civilization as codified by the first great agrarian kingdoms. As new and powerful societies, they were determined to distinguish themselves as sharply as possible from the populations from which they sprang and that still beckoned and threatened at their fringes. In its essential, it was an "ascent of man" story. Agriculture, it held, replaces the savage, wild, primitive, lawless, and violent world of hunter-gatherers and nomads. Fixed-field crops, on the other hand, were the origin and guarantor of the settled life, of formal religion, or society, and of government bylaws. Those who refused to take up agriculture did so out of ignorance or a refusal to adapt. In virtually all early agricultural settings the superiority of farming was underwritten by an elaborate mythology recounting how a powerful god or goddess entrusted the sacred grain to the chosen people.[17]

---

13. Sahlins, *Stone Age Economics*, 144.
14. James C. Scott, *The Art of Not Being Governed: An Anarchist History of Upland Southeast Asia.*
15. David Graeber, "Culture as Creative Refusal"; see also David Graeber, *The Utopia of Rules.*
16. Pack, *Meritocracy Mingled with Scripture.*
17. Scott, *Against the Grain*, 7.

The irony of Scott's claim here is that many people in the ancient world were not fooled by this propaganda. While some may have been suckered in by it and the often-monumental constructions of the cities, many resisted. Others sought to escape the cities to the "hills." As Scott points out, early agricultural civilizations spent far more time being attacked and falling apart due to internal strife than they existed in stability.[18] Even when they did become more established, there was a constant movement of people leaving or escaping cities and others being attracted to or captured by the cities.

This creates an odd ambivalence in texts like the Bible. On the one hand, there is an intense antipathy to Babylon and the great civilizations. On the other hand, some of the practices of nomadic warrior societies like patriarchy and the use of domesticated animals originate with these civilizations. Furthermore, with Kings David and Solomon, Israel itself became its own empire. Despite this, much of the text functions in the shadows of the pyramids, promising redemption from servitude.

The quickness with which we moderns, including anthropologists, have tended to dismiss hunter-gatherers as "primitive" and largely uninteresting is, of course, a reflection of the long-lasting hold of civilizational narratives on the imaginary "culturally advanced" traditions. There are layers to these pretensions of being more "civilized" than previous peoples.[19] The first layer begins with the Neolithic Revolution. A second occurs with the axial or classical age (800 to 200 BCE). A third, and the most self-assured of all, comes with the modern period. Even more than other "advances" in civilization, the modern era shifts our gaze to the future and away from the past. And the further in the past, the more uninteresting and backwards it must be for us moderns.

However, the rethinking in anthropology of the Neolithic Revolution radically challenges this narrative of progress. Instead of the longest period of human existence being one of starvation and wretched misery, which humankind finally began to leave behind with the discovery of agriculture, it appears that the longest period of human existence was one of abundance. At least until it was upset by the establishment of early agricultural civilizations. This introduced a fundamental scarcity into human experience.

---

18. Scott, *The Art of Not Being Governed.*

19. Justin Pack, *Prehistoric Philosophy: The Neolithic Revolution, the Indigenous Critique, and the Myths of Civilization*; see also Graeber and Wengrow, *The Dawn of Everything.*

Notice that this shift reverses when scarcity starts. In the civilizational narrative, scarcity exists from the beginning, an omnipresent threat that only starts to decline with the discovery of agriculture and the rise of early civilizations. But, in the Original Affluent Society (OAS) model, abundance is the norm for most of human existence, only to be replaced with scarcity after the Neolithic Revolution. Instead of a great leap forward, the Neolithic Revolution is quite the Pandora's Box, unleashing a whole host of evils.

The implications of this reorientation cannot be overstated. According to the OAS model, scarcity is not the norm. This means that scarcity is a problem we have introduced which requires ethical justification. Under the civilizational narrative, scarcity is a fact of life and does not require ethical justification. Yes, we can ameliorate some of the problems of scarcity, but ultimately it is here to stay and we will simply have to accept its omnipresence. God can fix it in the next life. This is the kind of reasoning that deludes us into accepting the many crude injustices of the status quo. It erases abundance from human history and places it in a possible future, exculpating us from any responsibility for current scarcity.

The entire tone of human existence shifts depending on how close or far we are from abundance. Abundance is safety, love, and fullness. This is why the narrative of progress is so attractive. It tells us that we have more in modern life than in any period before and that generally every day will be better. Some claim God has given it to us. The OAS model and the scriptural narrative disrupt the narrative of progress, however, by denaturalizing scarcity. The abundance we have is no longer compared with scarcity, but with an existential or divine abundance. Compared with these, our modern abundance suddenly appears impoverished. To clarify this, let's return to hunter-gather life and see how they created and preserved abundance. This will help show the difference between ideological modern abundance and the historical, lived, existential abundance.

Protecting Abundance

First, let's distinguish between the original abundance of hunter-gatherers and the divine abundance of scripture. Divine abundance can be miraculous, like Jesus multiplying the loaves and fishes to feed the 5,000. There is no natural explanation for how this happened. It is a promise and matter of faith. But there are also more mundane forms of divine abundance that are not necessarily miraculous in the same sense: the bounty of the earth, the rain, milk and honey, children, and so on. These things can be described as miraculous (including by nonreligious folks) but can also be described in naturalistic or scientific terms. The original abundance of hunter-gatherers is different from divine abundance because it is both natural and an accomplishment. It is therefore particularly important for defending the possibility of abundance, because it has nothing to do with faith and therefore cannot be facilely dismissed as something fantastical. In other words, skeptics can doubt divine abundance, but if anthropologists are correct, they cannot in good faith reject the existential abundance of pre-neolithic peoples. To be clear about what this means: for the majority of the existence of humankind, we did not live under the threat of scarcity. It is not natural; it is a human creation—or, perhaps more exact, the result of human failure.

What does it mean to say the original abundance of hunter-gatherers is an accomplishment? It means that hunter-gatherers were aware that if, as a community, they developed and enacted the proper cosmic civility by organizing themselves correctly and limiting certain dangerous behaviors, they could invoke the favor of the gods and preserve abundance. The key to understanding this is to recognize that the prehistoric world was full of gods and that everything in the world either was owned or patronized by a god or the embodiment of a god.[20] A wild boar is not just an animal but either a god or a creature protected by a god. The same goes for the water, the fruits, the birds, the wind, and so on. The gods are often willing to share with us, if we behave with civility towards them and their wards. (For example, the god that "owns" the boar may let us hunt and eat it if we show proper deference or perform the proper ritual.) If we just take whatever fruits we find without acknowledging and asking permission from the relevant gods, we risk stealing from and angering them. However, if we perform the proper rituals and recognitions and behave ethically, they will likely share with us.

This is probably not that far off from the way many Christians think about the Christian God. What differs in the prehistoric version is that there are many gods and they may have different requirements or expectations of how we should relate to them. If one came into contact with a new place or a new group of people, one would have to learn about the different gods of that place and their expectations. While the relationships with different gods would have varied, in general the primary form was gift relationships.

---

20. Marshall Sahlins, *The New Science of the Enchanted Universe: An Anthropology of Most of Humanity.*

Now, it turns out that gift practices can be complex and function in ways quite different from our modern understanding of gifting.[21] However, for the question of protecting abundance, let's keep it simple for the moment: gifts to the gods and appropriate civility toward their nonhuman and human wards recognize and honor them. When cosmic civility is shown, they are likely to share the abundance of the world with us. Then, based on what they give us, we should respond further. Thus, for example, if we are gifted a fish, we should return the bones to the river when we are done.[22] While the ritual practices will vary, the basic impulse is to always give back and always act with caution and respect.

This can be ruined by one idiot.[23] If one member of our community doesn't act with respect—say, by hunting and killing prey without the proper permission or ritual—they risk angering the gods not only with them, but with our entire community. We all may find ourselves punished for the negligence or hubris of one fool. Furthermore, while there may be an abundance of food, the greatest threat to that abundance may be one or a few humans hoarding it all for themselves and denying it to others. This is exactly what happens with chimpanzees. The alpha male will keep the best food for himself, bully others, and monopolize sexual access to the females. The alpha male lives high and impoverishes the others, both male and female.

What is amazing is that for the bulk of the existence of humankind, we resisted and crushed the wannabe alpha males that would wreck abundance by keeping more for themselves. Hunter-gatherers were not idiots. They knew there was a constant danger of these wannabe alphas taking power, and so they implemented various practices to prevent this from happening. For example, the San of the Kalahari will ridicule and verbally tear down any hunters that begin to brag about how great they are.[24] Furthermore, they construct practices intended to prevent good hunters from standing out too much. Hunters craft their own arrows and mark the arrows they make with their own name. However, they then trade their arrows with each other, mixing all of them up so that when a particular animal is shot, the arrow will likely not correspond to the hunter who successfully shot it, hopefully preventing good hunters from always

21. Marcel Hénaff, *The Price of Truth: Gift, Money and Philosophy.*

22. Lewis Hyde, *The Gift: Imagination and the Erotic Life of Property*, 26–27.

23. Tyson Yunkaporta, *Sand Talk: How Indigenous Thinking Can Save the World*, 24.

24. James Suzman, *Affluence Without Abundance: What We Can Learn from the World's Most Successful Civilisation.*

getting responsibility for the kill. Of course, the hunter may not get the message and may begin to act superior and push others around. If this is the case, it may become necessary to preemptively kill them.

Killing in such a situation may seem too much, but it reflects the hunter-gatherer understanding of the potential threat of wannabe alpha males. If they come to power, they may introduce domination and hierarchy into the community, disrupting not only the equality and freedom of the community, but also their abundance. In *Hierarchy in the Forest: The Evolution of Egalitarian Behavior*, Christopher Boehm argues that hunter-gatherers established a "reverse dominance hierarchy."[25] They establish egalitarianism to prevent "potential upstarts from dominating the rest. Egalitarianism is a form of dominance, the dominance of what Rousseau would have called the general will over the will of each."[26] In his evolutionary account of the rise of religion, Robert Bellah suggests that additionally, upstarts were curtailed through "the strong pull of social solidarity, especially as expressed in ritual, that rewards the renunciation of dominance with a sense of full social acceptance."[27] So strong were these community norms and intense preventative measures that "[w]e did not just suddenly go from nasty to nice. Reverse dominance hierarchy is a form of dominance: egalitarianism is not simply the absence of despotism, it is the active and continuous elimination of potential despotism."[28]

Interestingly, this is exactly what bonobos do. Unlike chimps, bonobos are led by an alpha female, but she maintains a social order that is much more egalitarian and peaceful than that of chimpanzees. She and her supports will, however, use violence on wannabe alpha males if necessary. Primatologist Vanessa Woods recounts a large male backhanding the alpha female of a group only to be attacked by five females, who gave him a good beating in response.[29] Like among hunter-gatherers, violence is being used to minimize violence. Domination is being used to minimize domination.

---

25. Christopher Boehm, *Hierarchy in the Forest: The Evolution of Egalitarian Behavior*, 10–11.

26. Robert N. Bellah, *Religion in Human Evolution: From the Paleolithic to the Axial Age*, 177.

27. Bellah, 177.

28. Bellah, 177.

29. Vanessa Woods, *Bonobo Handshake: A Memoir of Love and Adventure in the Congo*. See also her interview at Duke University, "Vanessa Woods on the 'Bonobo Handshake' {Duke University Office Hours}."

If Boehm and Bellah are correct, then the longest period of human existence was marked by a great egalitarian coup that established and maintained existential abundance and cosmic civility. It is likely we spent much more of our existence living like relatively peaceful bonobos than violent chimpanzees. Furthermore, this helps us see that scarcity arrives fairly late in human history, and that it only arrives with the unfortunate world-historical victory of the wannabe alpha male.

The Victory of the Warriors and the Rise of Civilization and Scarcity

As interesting and as critical it is, I will not attempt to recount the coup of the alpha males here. I have done so to some degree elsewhere and invoked better scholars than myself in trying to do so.[30] Rather, for our purposes here we need to take a moment to draw out the implications of what this means for our understanding of "civilization" and scarcity.

In the narrative of progress, the Neolithic Revolution was a leap forward in human history that allowed for the establishment of the first civilizations and the first move away from scarcity. The rethinking of the Neolithic Revolution overturns all this. Instead of starving hunter-gatherers jumping into agricultural work and the quality of life radically improving, the agricultural revolution was pivotal in the victory of the alpha males and the first step away from the abundance of pre-neolithic life. "Civilization" was the propagandistic name given by alpha males to the hierarchical states they established. By labeling everyone else as "primitive" and the new cities as "civilized," they were eventually able to establish a veneer of superiority and advancement that has remained into the present.

Of course, this pretension of superiority was rejected and ridiculed for a long time by many groups, including warrior cultures that themselves split off from agricultural civilizations. These warrior cultures were highly critical of the cities for their injustices and immorality (perhaps the most prominent example of this is the biblical lambasting of the "whore of Babylon"), but they also retained some practices. These included, most critically, patriarchy and the use of domesticated animals. Warrior cultures empowered and fundamentally shaped how we think of alpha males. This was due to their wild successes in founding axial traditions, including Judaism (and the later offshoots of Christianity and Islam), Greece and Rome, China, India, and so on. Each of these traditions begins with warrior cultures, and many with warrior epics that had profound historical influence (the Bible, the Mahabharata, *The Iliad* and the *Odyssey*). Even

30. Pack, *Prehistoric Philosophy*; see especially Scott, *Against the Grain*.

when some axial traditions rejected or resisted the glorification of warriors and warrior morality (such as Buddhism, Daoism, and the Cynics), it has remained a powerful influence on identity in these cultures.

From the perspective of pre- or non-neolithic peoples (hunter-gatherers), the lauded early agricultural "civilizations" represented the loss of abundance and the rise of scarcity, the establishment of dominance and hierarchy, the drudgery of agricultural work and the rise of slavery, human overreach in the cosmos (i.e., cosmic incivility), and the loss of freedom. From this point on abundance was only available to those on top, and those on the bottom often died exploited and starved. The biblical symbol of civilization was nothing less than Egypt and the pyramids, beautiful, awe-inspiring monuments to "alpha males" built by slaves. Even when Israel itself became an empire, the prophetic denunciation of civilization and inequality fills the Bible.[31] Much of humanity had lost abundance and fallen into the valley of scarcity.

Centuries later, there is an unsurprising parallel critique of modern civilizations, like the United States, from Indigenous peoples. Take for example the criticism that Native American Big Soldier voiced in 1820:

> I see and admire your manner of living, your good warm houses; your extensive fields of corn, your gardens, your cows, oxen, workhouses, wagons, and a thousand machines that I know not the use of. I see that you are able to clothe yourselves, even from weeds and grass. In short, you even do almost what you choose. You whites possess the power of subduing almost every animal to your use. You are surrounded by slaves. Everything about you is in chains, and you are slaves yourselves. I fear if I should exchange my pursuits for yours, I too should become a slave.[32]

Big Solider recognized the abundance of modern American society, but he rejected it because it is created through immoral means. American abundance is the result of the exploitation of both humans and nonhumans. Only those on top get to experience abundance; everyone else is forced to work through the fear of scarcity, through the fear of becoming homeless if one doesn't have a job. Modern abundance is impressive, but it is false. It is an illusion created through propaganda that erases those on the bottom. In Chapter 4, I will explore the frightful disappearance of the poor and downtrodden that is performed by contemporary meritocracy.

---

31. Abraham Heshel, *The Prophets*; Murray Bookchin, *The Ecology of Freedom: The Emergence and Dissolution of Hierarchy*.

32. Vine Deloria Jr., *Spirit and Reason: The Vine Deloria, Jr., Reader*, 4.

This chapter has sought to rattle us a little loose from the hold of the civilizational propaganda that asserts the omnipresence of scarcity. If we pay attention to the radical rethinking of the Neolithic Revolution occurring in anthropology, we discover that contrary to the narrative of progress, most of humanity has lived in a state of existential abundance, and this abundance was accomplished through attentive cosmic civility and careful and systematic repression of wannabe alpha males. This egalitarian coup in which humans established and preserved freedom and abundance was one of the great accomplishments in human history, but it was eventually lost after the Neolithic Revolution. This led to the current era of scarcity.

In the next chapter I want to continue the exploration of abundance by examining the logic of gift cultures and how that logic relates to the order of grace. We will examine the anthropological evidence and then combine and contrast it with scriptural claims.

2. The Order of Grace

In contemporary Christianity, grace is often taken to refer to the gift of salvation through the Atonement of Jesus Christ. While this is certainly the fundamental event in Christianity, I want to argue that this is a narrow understanding of what is meant by grace. Grace is more than salvation; it is an entire way of living, an order of grace. The language of grace is omnipresent in Latter-day Saint scripture, and it points not just to salvation but to a radically different way of living. In this chapter I want to articulate the logic of the order of grace, first by looking once again to anthropological evidence and then to scripture. My claim will be that this requires a radical reorientation toward grace on our part. It cannot be the mere acceptance of the gift of salvation; instead salvation comes through the grace-full order of gifting.

Gift Cultures

Early anthropologists repeatedly mistook the exchange of various objects by Indigenous peoples for "primitive" money. This was a projection of their own practices onto others and into the past. What they didn't realize is that money is a relatively new phenomenon. Before the axial age (800 to 200 BCE), most people did not have or use money. This was not because they had not invented it yet to streamline the process of bartering. They didn't barter either.[1] Simply put, they weren't economically minded. They were concerned with other things such as honor and recognition, ritual, play, enjoyment, hunting, gathering, and raising children.

In a very real sense, there was no economy—at least in terms of buying, selling, and exchanging goods.[2] Physical needs were taken care of through sharing and gifting. Gift relationships were widespread in prehistory. They existed between humans and gods but also between humans and other humans. We have to be somewhat careful when approaching gift relationships because there's a tendency to misunderstand them—apparent since Marcel Mauss's famous analysis of gift practices in his classic 1925 work, *The Gift*.

Mauss notes that gifting was a "total social phenomenon."[3] Gifting involved everyone, and it was ongoing. If A gives something to B, B will

1. David Graeber, *Debt: The First 5,000 Years*.

2. Sometimes anthropologists speak of "gift economies," but this is potentially misleading. It risks invoking money and trade when such things didn't exist or didn't function the way we tend to think they do.

3. Marcel Mauss, *The Gift: The Form and Reason for Exchange in Archaic Societies*.

be expected to give something back to A sometime in the future. This shouldn't be counterintuitive—we do it all the time with friends and family. As anthropologist David Graeber points out, if a friend needs help, we tend to help if we can. And we expect that if we need help, a friend will help us. This is what it means to be a friend, to care for each other.[4] What would be odd would be asking for help from a friend and having them offer to help us, but only if we pay back that help with interest.

In a world full of gods, gifting occurred not just between people but between people and the many different beings all around us in the natural world. While living in Indonesia, David Abram discovers his hosts leave a small pile of rice on a plate each morning for forest spirits. Later, he saw it being carried off by ants.[5]

Gifts can make friends of strangers. When the Spanish explorer Cabeza de Vaca was shipwrecked off the coast of Texas, he found himself living among Indigenous Americans for some time. When he finally left them, they gave him gifts. Then, when he arrived to the next group of people, he gifted them what he had been previously gifted. This showed them that he was human and friendly. They accepted him, and he lived with them for a period before moving on and receiving a goodbye gift. Over a period of years, he traveled from group to group across what is now the American southwest, gifting his way into and out of different communities until he was eventually able to travel all the way back to Mexico City.

However, and this is critical, gifts can be given with very different motivations. A gift can be given out of duty, to establish friendship, to maintain friendship, out of love, but also to manipulate others. It can placate a god, secure protection, or, more maliciously, humiliate others or force them into submission. The famous potlatch ceremonies of the Pacific Northwest were essentially parties thrown by the wealthiest, most powerful men and would feature them extravagantly raining gifts on all those who attended. But this was not out of kindness. To the contrary, these gifts indebted others to him. They would be expected to reciprocate with gifts at some future point even though it was already known they would not be able to, thus showing his supposed superiority and establishing control over others through his "generosity." In the Angami Naga of Assam, the wealthiest, most powerful man would organize a giant party in which he would distribute food and alcohol. The invited would be

4. Graeber, *Debt: The First 5,000 Years.*

5. David Abram, *The Spell of the Sensuous.*

expected to pay him back by helping transport a huge stone to the community and plant it upright as a symbol of his power.[6]

Thus, while we might be tempted to think of gifts as presents given out of love and care, the philosopher and anthropologist Marcel Hénaff argues this would be a misunderstanding of the primary use of gifts. They are neither economic nor given out of love. Rather, according to Hénaff, gifts tend to be part of agonistic games of recognition or honor.[7] There are two things to pay attention to here. First, these agonistic games would involve a whole community, like a potluck or the party of the Angami Naga or the ball games of Mesoamerica. This doesn't mean they were only about one person. Often, these agonistic games were ritualized and communal. One tribal leader giving a gift to another tribal leader would not be an exchange only about each leader, but about each community. Even though from one perspective it may look like they are being exploited by the powerful, members of the community might identify with their leaders and may root for them to "win." But also, while these rituals may be agonistic, like sporting events now, there might be a pleasure in the playing of the game. The onlookers are caught up in the rituals, the struggle, the victories, and the losses. And, as we've already seen, these games may involve not only those within the community; they also included those from other communities as well as the gods and other nonhuman beings all around us in the world. Agonistic gifting was thus a meaningful activity.

Second, Hénaff argues gift practices are focused on gaining recognition or honor. They are not about money or economic gain. In fact, as we see with the potlatch, the logic of gifting often works in opposite ways from the capitalistic logic of accumulation. Not accumulating but giving away is the name of the game. Of course, in doing this, the giver does accumulate honor and fealty. Or, to put the point differently and more starkly, the point is not an economic drive to accumulate money, but the drive to accumulate people (people who are indebted and must honor and serve their "lords").

For Hénaff there is an unfortunate tendency to see the ubiquitous gift practices of the past through a romantic or an economistic lens. Especially in twentieth-century French thought, no doubt because of the influence of Marcel Mauss, there was a strong desire to see in gift practices an alternative to the modern utilitarian obsession with money. While Hénaff rebuffs

6. Kant Flannery and Joyce Marcus, *The Creation of Inequality: How Our Prehistoric Ancestors Set the Stage for Monarchy, Slavery and Empire*, 104–9.

7. Marcel Hénaff, *The Price of Truth: Gift, Money and Philosophy*.

the romantic vision of gift practices, he does accede that gift practices do show that the modern vision of *homo economicus* is incorrect. Quite clearly, he thinks, the ethnographic evidence shows we are not naturally driven by a desire for profit, nor do we naturally think in utilitarian terms. The increasing tendency in economics to present human nature in these terms is therefore ideologically driven and false. To the contrary, we are a species that naturally cares and shares. In short, humans were, and can be again, grace-full.

If anything, Hénaff seems to be arguing we should learn from gift practices the importance of recognition for humankind.[8] He believes that modernity has completely failed to provide modern humans with an adequate sense of social recognition, and that this deep need was nurtured much better in gift cultures. While this topic is indeed very important, it takes us in a different direction than the purpose of this book and I will therefore leave it aside. Rather, what interests us here is the question of the order of grace, which Hénaff has claimed should not be read back into the history of gift practices. Is he correct?

Grace and Gifts

While Hénaff's analysis is very important to help us avoid reductive readings of gift practices, his analysis does not mean that some gift practices were not grace-full. If we recognize that gift practices were complex and were often agonistic, we can still learn much from grace-full gift practices.

Let's open the question of grace and gifts by looking at Lewis Hyde's phenomenology of art. Hyde is a poet, and his analysis is based on a simple but critical point about the experience of art. Hyde claims that his experience of poetry is that the poem comes to him. He doesn't make it up out of nowhere, and he can't force it into existence. Rather, he can create a kind of receptivity that will receive the poem if and when it comes. Where exactly does it come from? Hyde doesn't know, nor does he feel the need to know. From the muses, from a god, from the subconscious—artists have described this experience in different ways, but for Hyde what matters is that it is almost always experienced as a gift. Hyde quotes D. H. Lawrence: "Not I, not I, but the wind that blows through me."[9]

While Hyde doesn't leverage the language of grace heavily, it is clear that this gift of in-spiration (being breathed into) is not something that can be taken, forced, or earned. If it comes, it comes gracefully. And

8. Hénaff, 395–404.

9. Lewis Hyde, *The Gift: Imagination and the Erotic Life of Property*, xii.

because it comes as a gift, it results in a kind of ethical relationship. The particular inspiration, a poem in Hyde's case, must be treated with the proper care, respect, and gratitude merited because it is given freely. Poetic receptivity is a matter of openness, joy, and recognition. Interestingly, for Hyde it involves no known giver. It comes from wherever it comes from and the only sort of thing that can be done to "pay" for this—an unfortunately economic metaphor—is to treat it gracefully and to treat the space of receptivity gracefully. We could speak here of a graceful attunement.

Graceful attunement is often described in terms of love. Take for example this impressive passage from Robin Wall Kimmerer:

> Hold out your hands and let me lay upon them a sheaf of freshly picked sweetgrass, loose and flowing, like newly washed hair. Golden green and glossy above, the stems and banded with purple and white where they meet the ground. Hold the bundle up to your nose, find the fragrance of honeyed vanilla over the scent of river water and black Earth and you understand its scientific name: *Hierochlie odorata*, meaning the fragrant, holy grass. In our language it is called *wiingaashk*, the sweet-smelling hair of Mother Earth. Breathe it in and you start to remember things you didn't know you'd forgotten.[10]

Kimmerer is Potawatomi and a biologist. In her works she navigates the tensions between being a Native American and seeing the natural world as alive and personal, and her training as a scientist that tends to treat the natural world as mere objects. One of the remarkable things about her writing is her deep personal connection with plants and animals. The above passage is full of love, awe, and gratitude. Sweetgrass is not just organic material, but the "sweet-smelling hair of Mother Earth." Connecting with it through breathing it in (in-spiration) is a holy experience that makes her "remember things" she didn't know she had forgotten. What a remarkable divine experience! A similar ecstatic wonder and love fills her discussion of that lowly and oft-forgotten plant, moss.[11]

When I wrote a book about *amor mundi*, love of the world, a sensitivity reader pointed out that Native American writers and thinkers have been resistant to use the language of love to describe traditional Indigenous American relationships with the natural world or specific nonhuman beings in favor of the language of respect. This was because the English word "love" didn't fit the experience correctly and was too close to romance and the erotic. For example, one does not love a bear; one respects a bear. But

---

10. Robin Wall Kimmerer, *Braiding Sweetgrass: Indigenous Wisdom, Scientific Knowledge and the Teaching of Plants*, ix.

11. Robin Wall Kimmerer, *Gathering Moss: A Natural and Cultural History of Mosses*.

what is striking about Kimmerer's language is that it is not shy about having an aura of love and grace, while remaining rooted in respect. Another important Native American author that has adopted the language of love and grace to describe the Native American relationship with the earth, clearly inspired by Kimmerer, is Daniel Wildcat. He leverages this language as a foil to the mechanical, Western approach to nature and the resulting alienation and exploitation.[12]

Hyde argues the moral demand to be graceful is present in the Western tradition, particularly in traditional folktales. Here we find repeating tales of humans receiving gifts and then being punished or rewarded depending on how they respond to these gifts. Let me summarize one such tale to illustrate help see what Hyde is directing us to:

> Three sisters are old enough to leave their home. The mother asks the oldest if she would rather have a small piece of bread and her mother's blessing or a large piece and her mother's curse. The oldest sister opts for the large piece and the curse. Then on her journey she comes across a mother quail who asks the sister to share her bread with her and her babies. The sister refuses and is cursed a second time by the mother quail. Finally she arrives at a house where she is hired to look after a restless dead body. She falls asleep and is killed.
>
> The second sister makes all the same choices and is also killed in the end.
>
> The third sister opts for the small piece and her mother's blessing. She shares with the quail and both she and the quail eat to their fill and the mother quail blesses her. She is hired at the same house, does her job well and is given a potion to bring her sisters back to life.[13]

Here is how Hyde interprets this folktale:

> This story also gives us a chance to see what happens if the gift is not allowed to move on. A gift that cannot move loses its gift properties. Traditional belief in Wales holds that when the fairies give bread to the poor, the loaves must be eaten on the day they are given or they will turn to toadstools. If we think of the gift as a constantly flowing river, we may say that the girl in the tale who treats it correctly does so by allowing herself to become a channel for its current. When someone tries to dam up the river, one of two things will happen: either it will stagnate or it will fill the person up until he bursts. In this folk tale it is not just the mother's curse that gets the first two girls. The night birds give them a second chance, and one imagines the mother bird would not have repeated the curse had she met with generosity. But instead the girls try to dam the flow, thinking that what counts is ownership and size. The effect

12. Daniel Wildcat, *On Indigenuity: Learning the Lessons of Mother Earth*; see also Vine Deloria Jr. and Daniel Wildcat, *Power and Place: Indian Education in America.*

13. Justin Pack, *Money and Thoughtlessness: A Genealogy and Defense of the Traditional Suspicions of Money and Merchants*, 174.

is clear: by keeping the gift they get no more. They are no longer channels for the stream and they no longer enjoy its fruits, one of which seems to be their own lives. Their mother's bread has turned to toadstools inside them.

Another way to describe the motion of the gift is to say that a gift must always be used up, consumed, eaten. *The gift is property that perishes.* It is no accident that the gifts in two of our stories so far have been food. Food is one of the most common images for the gift because it is so obviously consumed. Even when the gift is not food, when it is something we would think of as a durable good, it is often referred to as a thing to be eaten. Shell necklaces and armbands are the ritual gifts in the Trobriand Islands, and when they are passed from one group to the next, protocol demands that the man who gives them away toss them on the ground and say, "Here, some food we could not eat." Or, again, a man in another tribe that Wendy James has studied says, in speaking of the money he was given at the marriage of his daughter, that he will pass it on rather than spend it on himself. Only, he puts it this way: "If I receive money for the children God has given me, I cannot eat it. I must give it to others."[14]

The first two sisters are selfish and act gracelessly. They do not appreciate what they are given and do not share it with the quail. Only the third sister adequately recognizes that she has earned none of what she has been given and that, as such, she cannot hoard it for herself but must share it. Here Hyde articulates a different account of gifting, one that we could perhaps call a graceful gift relationship. When the mother (A) offers the third daughter (B) a gift (A→B) she then leaves and has no opportunity to give something back to her mother (B→A)—except, perhaps, to then act gracefully. However, she soon has the chance to share this gift with the quail (C), thus moving the gift forward to another (B→C). Since the daughter has no chance to reciprocate with the mother, she does not set up a relationship of exchange but passes the gift on. There is no chance to calculate further potential benefits from paying her mother back, only the chance to continue the logic of graceful giving. Hyde argues that continuing the logic of graceful giving will eventually circle back on itself: C→D, D→E, and E→A. But this happening will be hindered if a calculative, strategic mentality inserts itself into this pattern of gifting. Hyde presents another folktale in which a fairy gifts a man a keg of ale that for years never runs dry. But when a curious maid opens it up, she finds spiderwebs and the ale never returns. Hyde concludes:

> The moral is this: the gift is lost in self-consciousness. To count, measure, reckon, value, or seek the cause of a thing, is to step outside the circle, to

---

14. Hyde, *The Gift: Imagination and the Erotic Life of Property*, 8–9.

> cease being "all of a piece" with the flow of gifts. . . . We participate in the esemplastic power of a gift by way of a particular kind of unconsciousness, then: unanalytic, undialectical consciousness.[15]

At this point the truly radical nature of Hyde's analysis emerges. With the discussion of folktales it becomes apparent that gifting is relevant not only to art but also to morality, and that strategy emerges as the enemy of both. Strategy here involves efforts to "count, measure, reckon, value, or seek the cause of a thing." This would include science, economics, business, contemporary ethics—our lives are so suffused with numbers, calculation, and strategy that it is hard for us to imagine how things could be done otherwise. But this is precisely what Hyde is trying to do: remind us that there is another way.

While it would be easy to dismiss Hyde's claims as romantic or unpractical, they are not rooted in speculative, fanciful thinking, but in compelling phenomenological descriptions of the process of making art and in historical common knowledge (folktales). If he is correct, he shows that even in our hyper-calculative modernity, there are pockets of grace-full practices left over from our past. This is clear in art, and it is clear in the morality of friends and family. As we saw with Graeber earlier, a friend is precisely someone with whom I don't act overly strategic. When a friend needs help, we tend to help them without calculating how it could profit us. We help them generously because we care for and love them. The same is often true with our close family members. It would seem odd to us if parents tallied up a tab over the course of a child's life and presented it to them with interest when they turned eighteen, or charged their children rent after the age of sixteen. These practices appear cruel and brutish, and yet we have built the rest of our lives on precisely this sort of behavior.

To be clear, Hyde is claiming much of our modern life is grace-less and unethical and is calling us to remember the logic of more human gifting practices that were widespread in the past. This claim is, I will argue, fundamental to Christianity.

Consider the Lilies

The obvious example of the Christian call to live grace-fully comes from the Sermon on the Mount in Matthew 6:

> Therefore I say unto you, Take no thought for your life, what ye shall eat, or what ye shall drink; nor yet for your body, what ye shall put on. Is not the life more than meat, and the body than raiment?

---

15. Hyde, 152.

> Behold the fowls of the air: for they sow not, neither do they reap, nor gather into barns; yet your heavenly Father feedeth them. Are ye not much better than they?
>
> Which of you by taking thought can add one cubit unto his stature?
>
> And why take ye thought for raiment? Consider the lilies of the field, how they grow; they toil not, neither do they spin:
>
> And yet I say unto you, That even Solomon in all his glory was not arrayed like one of these.
>
> Wherefore, if God so clothe the grass of the field, which today is, and tomorrow is cast into the oven, *shall he* not much more *clothe* you, O ye of little faith? (vv. 25–30)

These verses are perplexing to the modern capitalist mind. We are taught that scarcity is ubiquitous, and that there is not enough to go around so each of us has to think carefully and calculate how we want to secure our piece of the pie. The last thing we can do is "[t]ake no thought for your life, what ye shall eat, or what ye shall drink; nor yet for your body, what ye shall put on." This is a recipe for homelessness. When Jesus claims we should "consider the lilies of the field" and how they don't work for their survival, what are we supposed to make of this? He can't be serious, can he?

It is interesting to see how contemporary Christians respond to these famous passages, especially since it is presented as a challenge: "O ye of little faith!" In my experience, the primary responses to this challenge are either to ignore it or to turn it into something much less dangerous. One way this is accomplished is by holding on to the sense of grace for the blessing we are given while deemphasizing (dismissing really) the call to "take no thought" or "toil not." Surely these are hyperbolic! In Latter-day Saint circles, the relevant scripture that is regularly invoked is 2 Nephi 25:23: "For we know that it is by grace that we are saved, after all we can do." This verse is commonly used as a rejection of what is perceived as the evangelical emphasis on grace without work. Grace is preserved, but it comes after "all we can do." Thus, we should calculate and work, and then grace will put us over the top. As a result, what we end up with is the challenge to "consider the lilies" being reduced to the admonition to "calculate and work hard but recognize that what you are blessed with comes from God." However, if Hyde is right, this essentially dilutes what this challenge actually means and domesticates it into a more palatable, Protestant ethic–friendly admonition.

I would like to suggest that "consider the lilies" is an invitation to participate in abundance and the order of grace. On this reading, Jesus is telling us that abundance is real, scarcity is not natural, and that we should live according to the logic of grace. Like the Original Affluent Society model, Jesus asserts there is more than enough to go around and that we can see this abundance in the world around us in the very birds and flowers we witness everyday. This alternate order is not hidden; it is everywhere if we will just open our eyes to it. Doing so is scary, however, because so much of what we do is circumscribed by the fearful threat of scarcity and destitution. Have faith, Jesus says. God will provide. Stop overworking yourself; stop constantly calculating how to get further ahead, faster. Let go of these worldly concerns and turn to spiritual ones.

Notice that on this reading, there is still spiritual work to be done, and this may involve physical labor, but it will not be the toil of scarcity and inequality. The invitation to exit the world of scarcity for the world of abundance is also an invitation to exit the world of competition with our neighbors. We no longer need to or should be calculating how to get ahead of them. On the contrary, we should be sharing and caring for them. The invitation to exit the world of scarcity is also, then, the demand we stop coveting our own property.

Thou Shalt Not Covet Thine Own Property

The inversion of the invitation to experience divine abundance is the demand that we not covet our own property and instead help the widow and the orphan.

The command "[T]hou shalt not covet thine own property" (D&C 19:26) is an odd one, because we are not used to thinking of something that is ours as something that we can covet. Really this is a variation of the ubiquitous biblical reminder that nothing we own is ours but is rather a gift from God, upon whom we are dependent. As such, we should not hoard these things for ourselves:

> The earth is the LORD's, and the fulness thereof; the world, and they that dwell therein. (Ps. 24:1)
>
> Behold, the heaven and the heaven of heavens is the Lord's thy God, the earth also, with all that therein is. (Deut. 10:14)
>
> For by him were all things created, that are in heaven, and that are in earth, visible and invisible, whether they be thrones, or dominions, or principalities, or powers: all things were created by him, and for him. (Col. 1:16)

From a Christian perspective, even our body does not belong to us, having been redeemed (bought) by Christ:

> What? know ye not that your body is the temple of the Holy Ghost which is in you, which ye have of God, and ye are not your own? For ye are bought with a price: therefore glorify God in your body, and in your spirit, which are God's. (1 Cor. 6:19–20).

As such, nothing you own is yours, even if you "earned" it:

> And thou say in thine heart, My power and the might of mine hand hath gotten me this wealth. But thou shalt remember the Lord thy God: for it is he that giveth thee power to get wealth, that he may establish his covenant which he sware unto thy fathers, as it is this day. (Deut. 8:17–18).

Latter-day Saint scripture affirms our dependence on God and the necessity to not use the work we do to "earn" what we have as an excuse not to help others:

> And also, ye yourselves will succor those that stand in need of your succor; ye will administer of your substance unto him that standeth in need; and ye will not suffer that the beggar putteth up his petition to you in vain, and turn him out to perish. . . .
>
> For behold, are we not all beggars? Do we not all depend upon the same Being, even God, for all the substance which we have, for both food and raiment, and for gold, and for silver, and for all the riches which we have of every kind? . . .
>
> And now, if God, who has created you, on whom you are dependent for your lives and for all that ye have and are, doth grant unto you whatsoever ye ask that is right, in faith, believing that ye shall receive, O then, how ye ought to impart of the substance that ye have one to another.
>
> And if ye judge the man who putteth up his petition to you for your substance that he perish not, and condemn him, how much more just will be your condemnation for withholding your substance, which doth not belong to you but to God, to whom also your life belongeth; and yet ye put up no petition, nor repent of the thing which thou hast done. (Mosiah 4:16, 19, 21–22)

Furthermore, there is nothing you can do to pay God back for these blessings. We never leave this state of dependency. We never achieve "independence":

> I say unto you that if ye should serve him who has created you from the beginning, and is preserving you from day to day, by lending you breath, that ye may live and move and do according to your own will, and even supporting you from one moment to another—I say, if ye should serve him with all your whole souls yet ye would be unprofitable servants. (Mosiah 2:21)

This brings us back to the problem that opened this book. The problem of some keeping more for themselves and failing to share with others, thus creating inequality:

> For the earth is full, and there is enough and to spare; yea, I prepared all things, and have given unto the children of men to be agents unto themselves.
>
> Therefore, if any man shall take of the abundance which I have made, and impart not his portion, according to the law of my gospel, unto the poor and the needy, he shall, with the wicked, lift up his eyes in hell, being in torment. (D&C 104:17–18)

Taking of the abundance that God has made and imparting not our portion to the poor and the needy is, at least in this context, the original sin. All our problems stem from this: "[I]t is not given that one man should possess that which is above another, wherefore the world lieth in sin" (D&C 49:20). To be clear, keeping more of the abundance than one should is not just a sin against the poor; it is a rejection of the order of grace and divine abundance, which is to say, heaven. It is a rejection of heaven on Earth and is instead in favor of the hell of scarcity. If God's angry condemnation of those who keep more for themselves to hell and torment seems harsh, that should tell us something about our modern meritocratic dismissal of the poor, and it should key us into how much is at stake here.

The Order of Grace

Traditional folktales and biblical commandments insist on the moral need to share with each other. This is not only a concern for the poor and downtrodden (which is itself critically important), but also about the kind of world we live in. If we lose the sense that everything we have is a gift and begin to think that what we have is something that we have earned and therefore "ours," we will cease sharing and gifting and fall into a world of scarcity. Worse, we may come to see scarcity as natural and unavoidable. Once we move too far down this path, we find ourselves in a world in which it is every man for himself.

However, if we retain or reestablish a profound sense of the gift of life, we will not feel comfortable hoarding the abundance for ourselves. Living in a large house while others struggle to pay rent will appear evil. Wearing name-brand clothing while others wear rags will appear evil. Our very conceptions of wrong and right will shift radically.

This helps to explain the disparity between some of the things that God finds outrageous in scripture and what we tend to find outrageous in consumer capitalism. Rabbi Abraham Heschel puts the point this way:

> Instead of dealing with the timeless issues of being and becoming, of matter and form, of definitions and demonstrations, [the prophet] is thrown into orations about widows and orphans, about the corruption of judges and

> affairs of the market place. Instead of showing us a way through the elegant mansion of the mind, the prophets take us to the slums. The world is a proud place, full of beauty, but the prophets are scandalized, and rave as if the whole world were a slum. They make much ado about paltry things, lavishing excessive language upon trifling subjects.[16]

Again, this is not just about poverty; it is about the kind of world order we live in and the kind of logic we let rule our lives. Inequality is a foundational sin (D&C 49:20) not just because of the suffering of the widow and the orphan, but because it kills heaven on Earth and replaces it with the hell of scarcity.

I am hoping that the analysis I am offering helps to clarify the logic of grace and makes the order of grace a live problem. But these issues are also deeply clouded by what I claim to be the opposite of the order of grace: the order of money. When immersed in the logic of money, grace becomes hard to comprehend. To further illuminate the order of grace, it will help to expose the logic of money and the assumptions about individual responsibility, ownership, and relationships in consumer capitalism. Thus, in the next chapter I will turn to money itself and attempt to defamiliarize it—to show how weird money is. This was something that was very clear to axial philosophers like Aristotle and Plato. But money is also mystified by moral narratives like meritocracy. Thus, after we examine the weirdness of money in Chapter 3, we will have to look at meritocracy in Chapter 4. I have argued in a previous book that money encourages thoughtlessness.[17] While I will have to explain what I mean by this, it has become increasingly apparent that money doesn't just discourage us from thinking, but it also creates complicated institutional systems that require us to sell out our integrity and thus fundamentally compromise ourselves. We will turn to this problem in Chapters 5 and 6.

Once we have looked at the order of money, I will then return to the contrast between grace and money.

---

16. Hyde, 3.

17. Pack, *Money and Thoughtlessness.*

3. The Weirdness of Money

The first two chapters of this book discussed abundance and gifts with the purpose of offering a rough outline of the order of grace. Unfortunately, grace is often hard for us to understand because we have been raised to see scarcity as normal instead of abundance. Furthermore, many of our assumptions about what it is to be human, how we should act, how society works, and so on are shaped by the logic of money. We see the world through the lens of *homo economicus*. Thus, to better see grace, we need to examine how money shapes our thinking. Ultimately, I will be arguing that grace and money are opposed orders driven by fundamentally different logics.

In the remaining chapters of this book, I will turn to the order of money. In this chapter I will begin by seeking to denaturalize money, to defamiliarize it—to make it seem weird as it appeared to many axial thinkers like Aristotle and Plato. In the next chapter I will turn to the ideological system of meritocracy and how it provides a moral scaffolding to the world of money. In an earlier book, I explored the ways that money discourages us from thinking, or, to state the point differently, how it encourages one way of thinking at the expense of another,[1] but here I want to focus on how the abstract systems of consumer capitalism, driven by money, warp and morally damage us. This will be the topic of Chapters 5 and 6. With this background in place, we can return in the Conclusions to the fundamental choice we have to make: grace or money.

Traditional Proportional Economies

The first two chapters have already shown us a few things about money. First, for most of human history, money didn't exist. It simply wasn't needed. Second, people didn't barter (except perhaps quite rarely). A common assumption in economics is that money was created to streamline the potentially onerous process of bargaining. If one person has a chicken and eggs and another has bees and honey, and they each wanted some of what the other had, they would proceed to bargain: twelve eggs for a cup of honey, no, ten, twelve, ten, eleven, deal! But if one wanted honey but the other didn't want eggs, there was an impasse. When money was invented, it could be used to trade for anything, and problems with not

1. Justin Pack, *Money and Thoughtlessness: A Genealogy and Defense of the Traditional Suspicions of Money and Merchants.*

needing what another had to offer went away—we could exchange goods and services for cash.

But once we realize that for most of human history, we gifted instead of bargained, the question of why money was needed returns. The short answer (at least one of the main theories) is that money was an invention of the state used to bring populations under their control and maintain power over them.[2] This was first done by temples in Mesopotamia, but it became a widespread practice in the axial age (800 to 200 BCE). Greek city-states were obsessed with minting coins, and the Romans spread their empire by using them to pay their soldiers and then forcing conquered areas to accept the use of markets and Roman coinage: pay taxes to us and pay them in our coins.[3]

There are critical implications for the meaning of money, human nature, and social organization that follow from the model of money (and its origin) one accepts. In the economist model, money is merely a neutral tool that improves efficiency. It was adapted because thinking economically (trading and bargaining) is human nature. We are *homo economicus.* And since this is the case, it makes sense to organize society in ways that respond most appropriately to this natural economic disposition.

But, what if this is not the case? It means, among other things, that these misguided assumptions about human nature are being forced *on* us, not naturally found *in* us. We are being unnaturally shaped into *homo economicus*; we are colonized and deformed into economic beings when this is not our nature (or, at least, not our primary nature). It means that traditional practices, which are not shaped primarily by economic purposes, are being diminished and replaced by economic ones. And it means that money is not merely an innocent, neutral tool that improves efficiency, but an integral part of social control—both in the sense of control by a particular state, but also in the sense of the shaping of our minds and world by economic standards.

While this is hopefully apparent from the discussion of abundance and gift practices in the previous chapters, it will be worth it (an economic metaphor, many of which have infiltrated our language) to give another foil in addition to gifting. Specifically, we should briefly discuss traditional proportional economies.

To explain what I mean by a proportional economy, let's look at Christopher Clark's *The Roots of Rural Capitalism: Western Massachusetts*

2. Pack; see also David Graeber, *Debt: The First 5,000 Years.*

3. Graeber.

1780–1860.[4] Immediately, we should notice that this is not an account of ancient or "exotic" peoples. Rather, it is about rural communities in New England in the early 1800s. Perhaps surprisingly, Clark points out that these communities did not use money. Instead, they relied on IOUs, tabs, and memory. How did this work?

In a small rural community, everyone knows everyone. This fundamentally changes how we relate to each other economically. Say, for example, that I grow corn and my neighbor raises pigs (obviously this is simplified for the sake of making a point). We regularly exchange corn for pigs. But one year a disease that affects pigs sweeps through the community and many of my neighbor's pigs die. Knowing my neighbor's situation, I accept less from him than normal while continuing to provide him with some of my corn produce. I may be "losing out" in pure economic terms, but the pure economics take a back seat to the human. Two years later, when his population of pigs has rebounded, he "pays me back" by offering extra pigs as a part of our usual exchanges.

Notice that there is no set price for a pig or a bushel of corn. Rather, how much we exchange with each other depends on the personal and social circumstances of the moment. Suppose, to offer another example, there is a poor widow in the community. Her husband has died, and she has a hard time keeping up her with farm. Recognizing her situation, the members of the community may offer her more for less and accept things from her that they may not really need or want as "payment." If an epidemic has swept through the community and I have been the least affected, I may be more generous with others in light of these difficulties. Individual well-being and circumstances play a role in how we treat each other. Thus, the value of what we exchange is proportional to these circumstances. Cheaper for the widow. Cheaper for the individual who is dealing with a disease. More for a friend who has helped me out in the past. The economic is thus embedded and conditioned by personal and social situations.[5] All those involved will track what is happening and have a sense of who helped who, when, and to whom one may be indebted and want to "pay back" if possible. If doing so becomes complicated, IOUs and tabs can be used to help manage different "balances." Of course, there will be some people who take advantage of this in one way or another,

4. Christopher Clark, *The Roots of Rural Capitalism: Western Massachusetts 1780–1860*.

5. Karl Polanyi, *The Great Transformation: The Political and Economic Origins of Our Time*.

say, accepting kindness from others when needed but being stingy in their own exchanges, but this is also something that those in the community will be aware of. If someone is taking advantage of others, they will stop dealing generously with them.

So a proportional economy is one in which all these factors are taken into account, and exchanges are always run through this social matrix to establish proportional "prices." According to David Graeber, historically most local communities will tend to default to proportional, money-less economies unless they are forced into some sort of larger state that imposes money (and taxation) on them.[6] Thus, while it is common to understand narrative history as a series of empires, it is also possible to read history from the perspective of those who are able to return to money-less proportionality whenever they fall outside or on the margins of the influence of state power.

The Weirdness of Money #1: It is Abstract

Christopher Clark's account of proportional economies in rural New England in the early 1800s allows us to see the first strange feature of money: its abstractness. The purpose of Clark's book is not just to articulate traditional proportionate economic relations, but to also show how they are disrupted and fundamentally altered when money is introduced or reintroduced into them. Here is how Clark summarizes these changes:

> Cash payment connotes immediacy and a certain anonymity between dealers. Once a debt is paid off, obligation ceases. A debt paid off in cash implies abstraction—a social distance between buyer and seller. . . . Noncash payment and extended indebtedness entailed a different kind of relationship. Forms of payment had always to be negotiated, with due recognition of particular households' needs and abilities. Delays to payment resulted in perpetual, complex webs of credit and debt throughout the countryside that linked households to one another. Local exchange created networks of obligations alongside those already created by kinship or neighborhood.[7]

Money depersonalizes economics. It makes it an abstract exercise. It doesn't matter to whom I am selling my goods; the same price is offered to everyone regardless of their circumstances. The proportionality of traditional economies becomes anonymity and abstract equality. Murray Bookchin argues that "organic societies," which for our purposes here are societies with proportional economies, establish what he calls the "equality

6. Graeber, *Debt: The First 5,000 Years.*

7. Clark, *The Roots of Rural Capitalism*, 33.

of unequals."[8] He means by this that proportional economies take people who are at very different levels of capability, due to complex and varying circumstances, and balances them so they are at a "normal" or roughly equal level. Thus, the widow that is struggling to survive is given more and "charged" less precisely due to her disadvantaged situation. The "equality of unequals" tends to balance these differences out.

However, an abstract money-driven economy will result in what Bookchin calls the "inequality of equals."[9] Here each person is treated abstractly, like an atom—all the same, all stripped of personality and personal circumstances. All are treated as equal. But since all are equal, no proportional adjustments need to be made due to inequalities. If the results of economic exchange come out unequal, this is accepted as a just result for individuals starting from the same place. Thus, the result is the "inequality of equals." It is important to notice that this inequality is perceived as just, since everyone is treated in the same abstract fashion. Of course, to the widow who is left behind to fall into poverty this will not be experienced as justice.

Perhaps the best phrase to sum up the inhumanity of abstract money is the phrase: "It's not personal, it's just business." This is often invoked in situations when one person or company is leveraging economic power to crush another person or company but is insisting it is not being done out of malevolence since the whole process is abstract. The claim that money is abstract is a claim that says a world shaped by money will be an abstract world. The humans in that world will become abstract, which means they will be easier to exploit and ignore. It also means that they will tend to be alienated from themselves—to see themselves as an abstract object to be manipulated. Furthermore, the nonhuman objects in the world will become abstract and therefore easier to exploit. In an abstract world, plants and animals are increasingly seen and treated as objects that are potentially "useful" (exploitable) for us.

Another way of describing the shift from traditional proportional economies to abstract money economies is as a shift from qualitative to quantitative. Practical judgment that responds to particular circumstances is replaced by numbers. Human judgment could be fickle and mistaken;

8. Murray Bookchin, *The Ecology of Freedom: The Emergence and Dissolution of Hierarchy*, 219.

9. Bookchin, 224.

numbers are objective and universal.[10] Much like "it's not personal, it's just business," quantitative priorities defend what it entails with "this is just what the data says—numbers don't lie." When calculated correctly, they are just facts. There is no room to argue with them or get angry when they reveal something one might not like. Of course, numbers can be manipulated to warp facts, but if they are used properly or managed through a proper method—especially science—we should be able to trust them.

There are two things to notice here. First, numbers have become an object of intense faith in modern life. If we really want to convince someone of something, one of the most effective ways is to bring up some statistics that support our case. Thus, we often see academics and pundits throwing numbers at each other and, in the case of academics, arguing about methodology. Despite strong resistance to the ascension and rule of numbers and methods, quantification is quite entrenched as lord now.[11] Academic disciplines that are not primarily quantitative, especially the humanities, are in rapid decline. A second thing to note is that money and numbers work well together. Numbers games often slip into money games.

Of course, this brings us once again to the concern about the inhuman, abstract world that we are creating. For years, as an example, Mastercard has been running an advertising campaign that openly recognizes the conundrum. These *Priceless* ads, as the campaign is named, will present three consumer products followed by something touching, like spending time with a grandchild. Then the spokesperson will say: "There are some things money can't buy—for everything else, there's Mastercard." This is really quite a strange ad, because it pairs the ability to buy almost everything with the recognition that there are some things, the most important things, that cannot be bought (yet). This taps into our sense that there is something inhuman about an abstract system in which everything is reducible to commodities but which leaves a space for the qualitative and personal. While Mastercard is on the side buying and selling everything, consuming life and the world, it somehow recognizes the human core that cannot (yet) and should not (we shall see) be quantified and commodified.

This weird defense of the qualitative by a company driven by the quantitative is an *apropos* example of the bizarre place we find ourselves: slowly turning into machines, consuming our world around us, but being

10. Theodore M. Porter, *Trust in Numbers: The Pursuit of Objectivity in Science and Public Life*.

11. Without delving too far, one of the classic works on these issues is Hans-Georg Gadamer, *Truth and Method*.

seemingly incapable of thinking our situation through or slowing it down. We have film after film warning us about the dystopian society we are creating (*The Matrix*, *Treasure of the Sierra Madre*, *Blade Runner*, *Metropolis*, *Wall-E*, *Jurassic Park*—the list could be very long), but we are so caught up in overwhelming and accelerating changes that most are too busy trying to stay afloat to resist anything.

Lastly, it should also be mentioned that the abstract human, stripped of personal features, is a stranger. In embracing money, we enable the world to become abstract, and this turns it into a world of strangers. Sometimes this kind of concern is voiced as a criticism of cities from the perspective of rural communities where people "still know each other" and don't have to "lock their doors." However, the point is much broader than this. As we saw in the last chapter, many traditional moral imperatives and gifting practices are specifically designed to turn the stranger into a friend. The Bible unequivocally demands we take care of the stranger:

> And if a stranger sojourn with thee in your land, ye shall not vex him. But the stranger that dwelleth with you shall be unto you as one born among you, and thou shalt love him as thyself; for ye were strangers in the land of Egypt: I am the Lord your God. (Lev. 19:33–34).

In fact, Hans Jonas claims that traditional moral systems were based on face-to-face relationships, and that even with abstract moral systems like utilitarianism, we struggle to think and act ethically in a world in which we are interconnected in complex systems. We continue to fail to see how what I do here and now can affect someone far away much later. This is particularly evident, he thinks, in our failure to take the natural world into account and our failure to protect future generations of humans.[12]

The Weirdness of Money #2: Pleonexia

One of the weird things about abstract money according to Aristotle is how it can affect us. Unlike Plato, Aristotle isn't completely opposed to money. He claims trade is necessary for each household (*oikos*) and that money can facilitate household management (*oikonomia*—where we get the world "economy") as long as it is used properly.

However, for Aristotle, money is particularly dangerous because its abstract character makes it capable of bring accumulated to a much greater degree than other belongings. I can only own so many tables, but I can hoard many more coins. Since money can be used to buy many things, it

12. Hans Jonas, *The Imperative of Responsibility: In Search of an Ethics of a Technological Age*.

becomes extremely desirable—so much so that it often becomes an addiction, a disease. Aristotle calls this obsession with money *pleonexia*.

Now, many things can be addicting and therefore dangerous, like honor, sex, and war, but money is uniquely fungible and can be seemingly accumulated indefinitely. As such, it can create a particularly insatiable desire that seems to get caught in a very bad infinite. Both Aristotle and Plato believe that *pleonexia* is a critical threat to the democratic community of the *polis*, but also to our own souls. They would have learned this from Socrates, who, in his trial, famously harangued the jury (all of his peers in the *polis* that were present, which would have been hundreds of onlookers), claiming:

> Good Sir, you are an Athenian, a citizen of the greatest city with the greatest reputation for both wisdom and power, are you not ashamed of your eagerness to possess as much wealth, reputation, and honors as possible, while you do not care for nor give thought to wisdom or truth, or the best possible state of your soul?[13]

This is one of the most famous passages in the history of philosophy. Here Socrates claims that what should matter to us is wisdom, truth, and the well-being of our souls, but instead everyone is obsessed with money, fame, and power. Keeping in mind that one of the charges that had been made against Socrates was that he was guilty of corrupting the youth, we can see that what he is doing here is reversing those charges and claiming that it is not he, Socrates, who is corrupting the youth; rather, it is many of the esteemed citizens of Athens whose obsessions with money, fame, and power are destroying the integrity of the community and serving as a terrible example. Obviously, this didn't endear him to his peers, and he lost his trial.

A particular figure was emblematic of the corruption of character for Plato and Aristotle, and indeed, for much of the ancient world: the merchant.[14] Plato so detested the merchant that he banned them from the city he describes in the *Republic*. While Aristotle doesn't go this far, he did think merchants should only be allowed to enter and stay at the docks of the city. To let them further would risk having the pecuniary logic infect the rest of the community: the "power of money, when taken over by desire" can "release itself from the reciprocity of community relationships,

---

13. Plato, *Apology*, 29d-e.
14. Marcel Hénaff, *The Price of Truth: Gift, Money and Philosophy*.

to turn into unreasonable accumulation, and to move past the boundaries of the city." [15]

This extreme treatment of merchants comes as a surprise to many of us accustomed to capitalism, where entrepreneurialism is often celebrated. Why such antipathy to merchants?

The Weirdness of Money #3: Ontologically Unstable People (Merchants)

In the ancient world—not just in Greece—merchants were held in deep suspicion. They were often infected with *pleonexia*, and it warped their character in ways that many found profoundly disconcerting.

The problem is related to the nature of money. Aristotle famously claimed that money has the "unnatural" and alarming ability to give birth to itself, out of nowhere producing more of itself.[16] What Aristotle is pointing to is the way that the value of money (and commodities) can fluctuate unpredictably and irrationally. When I recently traveled to Mexico, I discovered that the exchange rate of Mexican pesos to American dollars was 20 to 1, whereas fifteen years ago it had been 10 to 1. The disparity meant that I could buy more with my exchanged dollars than made much sense to me. Furthermore, as a result of recent inflation, the prices of most things felt completely mixed up.

This weird shifting of value is part of what Aristotle is getting at. But probably the best example of money giving birth to itself is getting paid interest on loans, which was widespread even before the invention of coinage.[17] I could loan a neighbor some money with a high interest rate and six months later be given back twice the amount. The money doubled and I did nothing. If anything, Aristotle thinks, what I have sold is time—a very odd thing to sell. In fact, in medieval Europe, making loans was banned because it was seen as selling time—something that belonged to God. (Thus, only non-Christians, especially Jews, were able to engage in banking.)[18]

Money, then, was something very protean and strange. It seemed to be fundamentally unstable, and this instability would tend to rub off on the world and on those who dealt extensively with money: merchants. Let's

15. Hénaff, 78.

16. Hénaff, 87.

17. Michael Hudson, *...And Forgive Them Their Debts: Lending, Foreclosure and Redemption from Bronze Age Finance to the Jubilee Year*; Graeber, *Debt: The First 5,000 Years.*

18. Hénaff, *The Price of Truth.*

look at protean merchants first and then, in the next section, look at how money ontologically destabilizes the world.

Merchants are the human embodiment of the protean nature of money. It is as if money has rubbed off on them, recreated them in its own image. The basic point here is not hard to grasp: the merchant will do whatever is needed to make a sale. Today, the figure that fits this stereotype is the car salesman, although most settings that involve sales will also fit the bill. The image is that when you walk into a car shop, the salesman will often treat you like a friend, quickly approach, put his arm around you, ask how you are doing, and then say, "You look like you are looking for a convertible" while hustling you in the direction of one. If you say, "Oh, I was just looking for a restroom," the salesman will likely quickly remove their arm, point out where it is, and leave you alone. When you are a potential sale, they act the part of a friend. When you are not, they ignore you. Many of my students that have waited tables at restaurants report a similar phenomenon. They may be depressed, angry, or tired, but while they are in front of customers, they will put on a big smile and act friendly because this is the key to getting a good tip. If they don't put on a facade, they will likely get a smaller tip.

Put in the terms we were using earlier, the merchant (or the car salesman or the waiter) doesn't act like the stranger they are; they instead morph into a friend in order to gain some access to a proportional economic payment. We will often give or pay more to friends and family because we care about them. By simulating this kind of care, the merchant seeks to enter into a closer sphere than that of the stranger. They want to be treated like a friend. This, of course, is all feigned and quickly becomes apparent if you push the logic of friendship further, which I will admit, can be fun to do. When a salesman or a store acts like they genuinely care about you, ask them if they will give you what they are selling for free. They won't (unless perhaps they are a small mom-and-pop store) because your well-being only matters to the degree that it helps them make a sale. This is why the car salesman always acts like they are giving you an insider deal. It makes you feel like their friend who is getting special treatment because of that friendliness—but, of course, the discounts are already baked in. They aren't giving you a sweet deal; they are giving you the normal price that only seems like a deal because they had inflated the price in advance.

The merchant changes shape depending on the circumstances in order to maximize the chances of making a sale. In the past when merchants traveled between communities, this would mean potentially speaking different dialects, adopting certain customs—in short, trying to fit into each community they visited. The merchant was a stranger who could morph into a friend to one community and then morph into a completely different friend to another community. In itself, this might not be bad, but their status as a merchant made their moral motivation for doing so suspect.

Let me offer an interesting example. In Jean-Christophe Agnew's *Worlds Apart: The Market and the Theatre in Anglo-American Thought, 1550–1750*, he examines the reaction to mercantile or pecuniary logic breaking its traditional limitation to markets and becoming widespread in England. His approach is unique because he pays close attention to two traditionally delineated liminal spaces: the market and the theatre.[19] As we have seen, merchants were often understood to be actors, and like actors, they were dangerous and protean. Agnew claims medieval England had tightly proscribed social roles based on age, gender, class, and so on. Since these roles were established and stable, those who broke them or activities that broke them (like merchants, markets, actors, and theatres) had to be carefully limited in time and space. He points out that the phrase "the world is a stage" was initially used by churchmen to foster suspicion in churchgoers of the secular world, but after commodity exchange became increasingly normalized the phrase shifted to mean that everyone has to act more like protean merchants, whether they want to or not.[20] As more and more of life became up for sale, everyone had to increasingly deal with merchants who were moving far beyond their traditional spaces.

Not only were merchants more widespread, but the spread of markets meant that everyone had to act more like merchants. This meant a fracturing of the traditionally stable identities of the medieval era. No longer could I just be one person—I had to play multiple roles. Like an actor, each self now has a backstage where they prepare for their performances on the front stage. Interestingly, anger at the diremption of traditional roles and the new necessity to become previously suspect actors was directed at the theatre itself instead of at markets and merchants.[21] There was a series of riots directed at theatres during this period, although the anger was ultimately misguided. It was the markets and the spread of pecuniary logic that drove these changes, not Shakespeare.

19. Jean-Christophe Agnew, *World Apart: The Market and the Theater in Ango-American Thought, 1550–1750*, 23, 40.

20. Agnew, 16.

21. Agnew, 104.

The Weirdness of Money #4: An Ontologically Unstable World

In the changes in England that Jean-Christophe Agnew outlines, we see that it is not just individual characters that are warped by money; in a very real sense the entire social world is. Ultimately, the protean nature of money can affect the ontological stability of the world itself. Let me offer two examples of this from Stephan Eich's analysis in *The Currency of Politics*.

The first example is the financial crisis in England in the 1690s and the great recoinage of 1696. Many factors played a part in this crisis, especially England's ongoing wars with France. For the influential philosopher John Locke, another part of the problem was that the country's coinage was in disrepair. Under the influence of Aristotle, money had long been considered in Europe to be a dangerous source of instability. Locke essentially agreed with this, but instead of trying to get rid of it, Locke wanted to lock money down, to stabilize it. Money was like language, he thought.[22] If language is not used precisely and carefully, it can become fuzzy, inexact, and confusing. It can become a force of misunderstanding and obfuscation, doing so outside of human intention. Money is similar. And this was, Locke argued, the problem in England.

During the time Locke was writing, silver coins were often clipped and mangled to steal off bits of valuable metal from them. A clipping here, a cut there, left many of the coins misshapen, beaten, and worn. (The ridges on many coins today are a relic of this, as they were added to prevent persons from shaving metal from the sides.) Oddly, even a clipped and mangled coin was supposed to be worth the same value as an unclipped one. They are ostensibly both units of the same currency. Their equal value, despite their different states (one degraded and diminished, one not), points to the ultimate arbitrariness of their value. If they are worth the same, it is because of state decree or social acceptance of their value.

This could not be, Locke asserted. The coinage needed to be fixed and standardized in value, and that value with the metal that made up the coin. Clipping coins needed to be considered a crime—but not just a crime of theft, a crime against the ontological stability of reality itself. In fact, when Locke's good friend Sir Isaac Newton (yes, that Sir Isaac Newton) was put in charge of the royal mint and tasked with bringing about the great

22. Stefan Eich, *The Currency of Politics: The Political Theory of Money from Aristotle to Keynes*, 63–66.

recoinage, he actively sought to prosecute and even execute those who would defile the new coins.[23]

Coins were about trust. Stable, confident coins, like stable, unambiguous language, could serve as a foundation for a stable, confident society. Eich claims that Locke knew this was an illusion, a necessary lie. Since it was not in the nature of money to be stable, it was all the more important to make it seem like money was solid and grounded in the unshakable value of precious metals. While we now see the price of silver and gold fluctuate, Locke treated their value as if they were eternally set in stone. When coinage was tied to these precious metals, it participated in this eternal stability. Eich claims this illusion "profoundly altered the way subsequent generations understood money."[24] Even in the present day, there are those who see some kind of inherent value in gold and silver and will "invest" in them when confidence in currency or markets are low. For Eich, this represents a "depoliticization" of money. By this he means that by trying to create the illusion that money is fixed and stable because it is tied to eternally valuable precious metals, Locke is essentially trying to get us to not pay attention to money at all. It is, we are now told by economists, merely a neutral tool. Money in itself implies nothing political or social; it is only the way it is used that matters. This is, of course, more delusion.

It was under this pretension that Newton oversaw, starting in 1696, the collection of all coins, their reminting into new coins, and the rigid enforcement of prohibitions on clipping. Perhaps surprisingly, only one hundred years later, at the turn of the nineteenth century, England began experimenting with a new form of money that had critical implications about the ontological stability of money: paper money.

In 1797, Britain suspended the gold standard and started printing paper money. Often associated with the beginning of the financial revolution in Europe, this seemingly signaled a rejection of Locke's fixation with stable coinage. In fact, Britain had already been experimenting with government bonds, which were essentially a way for people to give money to the government as an investment that they could cash in later after the value of the bonds hopefully appreciated. As David McNally argues, this was essentially a bet that the government would be able to continue to extract more wealth and labor from its own populace in the future.[25] This became a way for a government to raise money for itself, most often

23. Eich, 68.

24. Eich, 73.

25. David McNally, *Blood and Money: War Slavery, Finance, and Empire.*

to fund war. This was speculative, essentially betting on the future. Like Aristotle had claimed about earning money on interest, this was essentially selling time or making money doing nothing. (The money just gave birth to itself.) Instead of this being seen as a threat, it was seen by speculators and some members of government as an opportunity. Instead of trying to stabilize and clamp down on the plastic, protean powers of money, they chose to take advantage of these characteristics. If money is not fixed and can be whatever we want it to be as long as we can achieve or force social acceptance of this, we can seemingly create value out of nowhere!

This was what alarmed critics of financial capitalism. The weird instability of money was leveraged to create more of itself. Money out of nothing seemed to imply that, at bottom, money was nothing, and if money was nothing, perhaps everything was nothing?

The German philosopher Johann Gottlieb Fichte argued that these new powers of financial capitalism to create value seemingly out of nowhere should be marshaled for the benefit of Prussia. What needed to be done was create a "closed commercial state" (this was the name of the book he wrote arguing for it).[26] If a state could isolate itself from outside markets, he argued, they could essentially create value by fiat. The British government had simply started printing paper money and, to everyone's surprise, it hadn't affected the value of British currency (although this experiment was drawn to a close shortly after by tying paper money to precious metals). Note that his argument is based on the unstable nature of money and its weird ability to give birth to itself. As long as a particular state government was strong enough to enforce social norms about the value of money, it could essentially make everyone in the state richer. Money, if controlled, could serve the well-being of the state.

Whether or not this would have worked, what is important is to see that Fichte had started like Locke, with the instability of money; however, unlike Locke's conclusions that we need to stabilize money to stabilize reality, Fichte argued that we can use the techniques of financial capitalism to harness the instability of money to improve the material conditions of society. In other words, we should take advantage of the ability of money to destabilize reality in order to remake it in a better way.

Eich claims that Fichte's arguments were too radical and that the implications of his claims were too strange and frightening. He seems to imply that reality is whatever we make it to be, and that money, managed in a closed commercial state, can do all sorts of strange miracles. In England,

26. Eich, *The Currency of Politics*, 94.

while financial capitalism took off, the Lockean ideology of stability remained in place—it was as if the idea of an unstable reality was too dangerous, so any games of financial capitalism by government had to be kept on the ideological low down. The wealthy, of course, could play whatever games they liked. Thus, while in many ways the door to play with money was opened, the official doctrine about money remained rooted in the gold standard.

Almost two hundred years later when Richard Nixon took the United States off the gold standard, money was left to float freely, essentially retaining its value based on the reputation and global power of the American dollar.[27] Now there are digital forms of money that are tied to nothing at all except whether modern society or a particular community accepts them. Here the irrationality of speculation meets with the juvenile in Dogecoin, Guncoin, Pandacoin, and PooCoin while the deadly serious game of making money thumbs its nose at honest work. Who bothers with earning money when you can get rich goofing around?

Money as a Religion: Market Triumphalism

It is remarkable that the bizarre absurdities of cryptocurrencies are tolerated. It should be pointed out that they are experienced as disconcerting not only because of their irrationality, but also because of how they directly undermine the ideological narrative of meritocracy. By meritocracy, I mean one of the most prominent and widespread ways of making moral sense of the world in consumer capitalism. At its most basic, it is the idea that hard work leads to success. This simple principle is the foundation of an ideological system that for many provides their sense of identity and moral goodness ("I worked hard so I am a good person who deserves what I have"). I will turn to meritocracy in the next chapter, but for the moment what I want to point out is that cryptocurrencies are directly at odds with the basic meritocratic principle of hard work leading to success. Despite this blatant and clear contradiction, there is only minimal concern voiced about cryptocurrencies. Why this failure to see the threat of cryptocurrencies to the moral narrative of meritocracy? The short answer is the final weird feature of money that I want to address in this chapter: money, and the ideological systems that support it, can become a religion.

Aristotle and Plato worried that *pleonexia*, the addiction to accumulating money, would crowd out traditional morality and replace commitments to the *polis* and the good life with a stultifying, endless quest for

27. McNally, *Blood and Money*.

ever more money. A similar concern about money was evident in Judaism and Christianity (indeed, with almost all the axial traditions). The ability of money to take over our institutions and our souls meant that it needed to be carefully delineated and controlled.

Modernity has rejected the traditional limits on money and markets, and we now find ourselves in a situation in which money and the social institutions and moral frameworks that enable it have become divinized in some circles. Take for example what the religious scholar Harvey Cox found when he started reading the business sections of various newspapers:

> Instead I was surprised to discover that most of the concepts I ran across were strangely familiar. Expecting terra incognita, I found myself instead in the land of déjà vu. The lexicon of the *Wall Street Journal*, *Financial Times*, and the *Economist* turned out to bear a striking resemblance to Genesis, the Epistle to the Romans, and Saint Augustine's City of God. Behind descriptions of acquisitions and mergers, monetary policy, and the convolutions of the Dow and the NASDAQ, I gradually made out the pieces of a grand narrative about the inner meaning of human history, why things go wrong, and how to put them right. Theologians call these myths of origin, legends of the fall, and doctrines of sin and redemption. Here they were again, and in only thin disguise: chronicles about the creation of wealth, the seductive temptations of over-regulation, captivity to faceless business cycles, and, ultimately, salvation through the advent of free markets, with a small dose of ascetic belt-tightening along the way for those economies that fall into the sin of arrears. I realized then that my many years of studying religion and theology had prepared me to approach this mysterious thing called the economy more knowingly than I could have guessed.[28]

Alarmingly, Cox finds that the economy has been divinized, taking over traditional Christian narratives and incorporating them into its own narrative of money as salvation. Eugene McCarraher has traced the rise of capitalism in the United States and concludes: "[C]apitalism is a form of enchantment—perhaps better, a *mis*enchantment, a parody or perversion of our longing for a sacramental way of being in the world. Its animating spirit is money. Its theology, philosophy, and cosmology have been otherwise known as 'economics.'"[29]

Lee Boldeman argues that the academic discipline of economics in particular has surrounded these changes with an air of scientific and religious universal truth, establishing themselves as the venerable priests of money:

---

28. Harvey Cox, *The Market as God.*

29. Eugene McCarraher, *The Enchantments of Mammon: How Capitalism became the Religion of Modernity*, 5.

[E]conomics threatens to become the dominant rationalist and fundamentalist religion of contemporary capitalist society and of the emerging global civilization. This threat is aided by its attempt to appropriate the prestige associated with the natural sciences. Importantly, it is easy to slip between the uses of individualism as an analytical tool to a promotion of individualism as a normative ideal. This religion is of particular appeal to business and political elites because it tends to legitimize greed, love of money and power. It is leading to the commercialization of all human activity, while aiding the atomization and privatization of competing values and groups. It has elevated money beyond a convenience to the means of salvation and the source of meaning, values and security, turning it, and the mechanism for acquiring it, into idols.

Economists—the prophets and priests of this new religion—preach about and have a major impact on public policy and our institutional arrangements. Economics therefore provides an alternative faith tradition, complete with values, ideas of welfare and of progress—usually defined in terms of quantitative economic indicators, which dominate public discourse and which seek to reshape our institutions and organizations. With their influence on government, economists are the new theocracy, the contemporary manifestation of Plato's guardians. In particular, the economic theologian's rhetoric resembles contemporary process theology. In this school, although God will possess the classic attributes of omnipotence (all power), omniscience (all knowledge) and omnipresence (present everywhere), He does not yet possess them in full. Such a theology offers considerable comfort to the economic theologian, explaining the dislocation, pain and disorientation that are the results of transitions from economic heterodoxy to free markets. THE MARKET is becoming more like Yahweh of the Old Testament: not just one superior deity contending with others, but the Supreme Deity, the only true God, whose reign must now be accepted universally and who allows no rivals. There is no conceivable limit to THE MARKET's inexorable ability to convert creation into commodities. In the church of THE MARKET, everything—no matter how sacred—eventually becomes a commodity. This radical de-sacralizing dramatically alters the human relationship to land, water, air and space. Indeed, human beings themselves start to become commodities as well. . . . THE MARKET has become the most formidable rival to traditional religions, not least because it is rarely recognized as a religion. The contradictions between the world-views of traditional religion and the world-view of THE MARKET religion are so basic that no compromise seems possible.[30]

There is a lot happening here, but the basic point is that money and the modern economy have become a religion. From a secular perspective, these warnings are meant as a threat: a new and dangerous cult is breaking

30. Lee Boldeman, *The Cult of the Market: Economic Fundamentalism and its Discontents*, 279.

the bounds of the separation of church and state and imposing a god on us right under our noses. From a religious perspective, these are claims that religion is being hijacked by a false god: money.

To better understand what is happening, we need to understand that contemporary money functions within a moral framework of meritocracy. This framework shapes how we understand money and its accumulation. In other words, it lends money a moral aura and provides the moral rationality for a world of money. Once we flesh this out further, we will be able to better see how cryptocurrencies and, more fundamentally, money itself both threaten our meritocratic ideals but also give away the game, revealing the grotesque contradictions at the heart of one of our primary forms of moral identity.

4. Meritocracy

Money has never existed in a vacuum, especially since most human societies never had a need for it. This means that any society that did use money needed some degree of justification for doing so (patriotism, social control, imperialism, and so on)—especially in light of the weird aspects of money we examined in the previous chapter. In this chapter, I want to articulate meritocracy as the primary contemporary system for justifying the use of money and show how this system takes something that was traditionally treated with immense suspicion and sublimates it into the engine of a supposedly just social order.

To do so, I will build on the argument I made in *Meritocracy Mingled with Scripture*. There I argued that meritocracy is not merely a political doctrine but has become a theodicy—an explanation of why evil might be allowed by an all-powerful and all-loving God. In other words, I agree with the concerns of the authors at the end of the last chapter: meritocracy functions like a religion. Except, by framing the issue in terms of meritocracy and not just markets and economics, we can see the way that our self and social identities and our very sense of moral goodness become tied to work and money. From a Christian perspective, this displaces the promise of justice from the next life to this one. It steals God's promises and delivers them here and now. It is, in short, idolatrous.

I'll begin by offering a summary of the argument in *Meritocracy Mingled with Scripture* to show that meritocracy is not just a political system, but a moral one. Then we will look at Michael Sandel's important critique of meritocracy. Last, we will look at the significance of "honest work" for the pretensions of meritocracy.

Theological Meritocracy

The basic idea of a meritocracy seems simple: those who have "earned it" should rule. Or, a slightly different version, those who have proven to be the most competent should be in charge. This is in opposition to an aristocracy in which positions of leadership and power are essentially hereditary, despite the word "aristocracy" itself meaning the rule of the best or the superior. Meritocracy is seeking for the same thing, but it insists that rule must be achieved rather than born into.

While the term "meritocracy" points to politics, the contemporary understanding of what is entailed by it is, at its core, about morality. We could therefore speak of politically focused meritocracy and morally focused meritocracy. This is not meant to indicate that there is not a moral component in politically focused meritocracy. Notice the ethical "should" in the definition of meritocracy offered above: those who have earned it *should* be in charge. And indeed, politically focused meritocracy will also often emphasize things like efficiency and other utilitarian values. Rather, I would like to claim that meritocracy can be tied to the moral goodness of each individual (and by extension society as a whole) and not just by desirable political results.

The more overtly morally focused meritocracy tends to see the political "should" as being rooted in a more fundamental "should" that is often articulated in terms of work or labor: success *should* follow from hard work. This more fundamental "should" can be heard in different ways and can come into conflict with the more strictly political meritocracy. For example, suppose we have two math students. One struggles with math but works really hard and is fairly successful. The other just seems to have a knack for math and is able to put in minimal work but consistently get the best results. If we are seeking to create some new technology, we may likely hire the naturally talented individual over the hard worker. But this is frustrating from the perspective of moral meritocracy, because the moral claim "success *should* follow from hard work" is much more than just a claim about what is efficient or produces the best results. It is a claim that success should be worked for, not born, lucked, or talented into.

This strong emphasis on work is central to the ideological vision of contemporary meritocracy. Emphasizing work and not just luck or talent means that success should be an achievement. It should be something that is earned. It is something that we have control over and therefore something that we are responsible for. This is something many now find somewhat intuitive, and it is important to note that it is directly in conflict with the logic of grace—which says nothing is earned and everything is a gift. Why is work or earning so important to our contemporary sense of what is fair?

My answer is twofold. First, meritocracy has become a theological system. Second, meritocracy as theodicy gives many their sense of moral identity—it tells us who is good and who is bad. If this is correct, meritocracy has become far more than a political system. It is functioning like a religion. Let's look at how.

First, how is work the lynchpin of theological meritocracy? We see "hard work" constantly appealed to as a justification for our contemporary inequalities. Those who are wealthy often appeal to how hard they have worked for what they have: "It took me years of hard work to be able to afford this nice house and no one can take that from me—I earned it." It is really important to notice that the claim "I earned it; I don't have to share" only makes sense if we accept the inverse: those who do not have must not have worked hard and don't deserve to be shared with. They had their chance. The inequalities of modern life are not unjust; on the contrary, inequality is a form of justice. I earned what I have by working hard. They must not have worked hard, so they don't deserve to have the same as me. They deserve to be poor.

To understand the world this way requires a critical shift. "Success *should* follow from hard work" has to be changed to "success follows from hard work." Here an ethical ideal has changed into a statement about reality. If the ethical ideal can be transmuted into ontological reality, we end up with a powerful meritocratic system that justifies the inequalities of the contemporary social order. It becomes a defense of the current social order and, for some, a theodicy—a defense of God. Meritocracy justifies existence: this world is not evil, everything happens for a reason.

Second, this sort of theological meritocracy has profound implications for our sense of social and self-identity that help explain why it is embraced and defended so rigorously. A good person in this kind of meritocracy is a person who has worked hard. Success follows from hard work. Therefore, a successful person is a good person. A bad person in this kind of meritocracy is a person who has not worked hard. Since they have not worked hard, they will not be successful. Therefore, an unsuccessful person is a bad person.

Now, both of these claims are obviously fallacious. There are many people who work hard and don't succeed due to many possible factors, including bad luck or structural disadvantages (such as racism or sexism). Inversely, there are people who are successful who haven't worked for it. Frustratingly, this tends to be ignored because if it were to be the case, the moral system that justifies our inequalities would fall apart. We often find those who are successful claim to be so because of hard work, even when it is not the case. More insidiously, we often find that many just seem to assume that those that are successful must have worked hard to get where they are, because that is how things work and, critically, if they haven't then the whole ideological system threatens to fall apart. In other words, we connect hard work with success because this pretension is central to our contemporary self-identity: I am a good person because I work(ed) hard. If this meritocratic system is not true, then the ground of my sense of moral esteem would crumble. All the more reason to insist that meritocracy is real—otherwise what am I? The result is a system of social and self-understanding that is clearly delusional but held on to tightly by many of those involved because of the supposed justice and moral identity it provides. Many who are wealthy want to believe they worked hard and are good people, regardless of whether they have or not. They also want to believe that poverty is the result of a choice, and, as such, the wealthy do not have moral responsibility to share with the poor. They can earn it too—if they want it. Oddly, many who are poor defend this system also, because they want to believe that, even though they may have worked hard and it has not led to success, it will happen soon. They hope that if they keep working hard, their time will come, even though this hasn't proven true so far.

Theological meritocracy is, then, riddled with tensions—tensions between itself and political meritocracy—which don't always align perfectly. There are internal tensions and resentments that it builds between classes and individuals, as well as tensions between itself and older theological systems that are at odds with it. As we saw in Chapter 1, the egalitarian communities of early humankind did not tolerate those who did not share with the rest of the community and instead hoarded abundance for themselves. Such hoarding was not just immoral; it was also a danger to abundance and the community itself. Such wannabe alphas were ridiculed, put in their place, and, if necessary, killed. But—and this is critical—the contemporary moral anger is most often not about inequality, but unearned inequality. Meritocracy is precisely about rewarding those who work hard and perform the best. Those who do so are assumed to deserve power and prestige, and everyone else should not be upset or jealous of their unequal station. Those who don't work hard deserve to be poor.

This is how we end up with Christians that laud and defend the rich instead of condemning them, and condemn and ignore the poor instead of helping them. Up is down; down is up.

In *Meritocracy Mingled with Scripture*, I approach these issues from inside Christianity to observe the infiltration of the gospel by this alternative religious system. However, the issue can be viewed from a secular social and political position as well. This is what Michael Sandel does in his *The Tyranny of Merit: What's Become of the Common Good?* From this perspective, what we find is not an infiltration of religion; rather, we find something more like an attractive political system that imports a hidden and damaging theology. On this model, it is a warped version of Christianity that invades and damages our social and political organization. While my account was shaped by his, it is worth going over his argument to further clarify the fundamental role of identity and moral goodness to meritocracy.

Sandel's Critique of Meritocracy

One of the odd things about meritocracy is that everyone, both politically left and right, seems to agree it is the correct ideal. What they disagree about is the degree to which we are already a meritocracy. In the United States, for example, Republicans tend to believe the country is already a meritocratic society. When the governor of Florida's general counsel was asked to define "woke," he said it means "the belief there are systemic injustices in American society and the need to address them."[1] He didn't deny there are inequalities, he denied they are unjust. The inequalities are just. Everyone gets what they deserve in a righteous meritocracy. Democrats, on the other hand, tend to believe that the United States is not yet a meritocratic society and that there are many systematic forms of discrimination that are in the way. To become a more meritocratic society, we would need to address racism, sexism, transphobia, and so forth. This would involve a multipronged effort that might include policies such as affirmative action, stronger penalties against discrimination, and better education.

While this fundamental disagreement about whether the United States is currently a meritocracy produces drastically different political policies and programs, Sandel argues that both share a commitment to the ideal of meritocracy. But, he claims, this is a mistake:

> What if the real problem with meritocracy is not that we have failed to achieve it but that the ideal is flawed? What if the rhetoric of rising no longer inspires, not simply because social mobility has stalled but, more fundamentally, because helping people scramble up the ladder of success in a competitive meritocracy is a hollow political project that reflects an impoverished conception of citizenship and freedom?[2]

To clarify his concerns, Sandel asks us to imagine a society that is a fully actualized meritocracy. This would mean eliminating biases, discriminatory social structures, and anything else that impedes social mobility. Now, on the one hand, the resulting meritocracy would seem to be a very good thing:

---

1. FOX 13 news staff, "What Does 'Woke' Mean? Gov. Desantis Officials Answer During Andrew Warren Trial."

2. Michael J. Sandel, *The Tyranny of Merit: What's Become of the Common Good?*, 120.

> A perfectly mobile society is an inspiring ideal for two reasons. First, it expresses a certain idea of freedom. Our fate should not be fixed by the circumstance of our birth but should be ours to decide. Second, it gestures to the hope that what we achieve reflects what we deserve. If we are free to rise based on our own choices and talents, it seems fair to say that those who succeed deserve their success.[3]

But, on the other hand, it would allow for and entrench some deep divisions in society:

> To begin, it is important to notice that the meritocratic ideal is about mobility, not equality. It does not say that there is anything wrong with yawning gaps between rich and poor; it only insists that the children of the rich and the children of the poor should be able, over time, to swap places based on their merits—to rise or fall as a result of their effort and talent. No one should be stuck at the bottom, or ensconced at the top, due to prejudice or privilege.
>
> What matters for a meritocracy is that everyone has an equal chance to climb the ladder of success; it has nothing to say about how far apart the rungs on the ladder should be. The meritocratic ideal is not a remedy for inequality; it is a justification of inequality.[4]

This is a point I emphasized above. Meritocracy does not only encourage inequality; meritocracy sublimates it. It turns inequalities into signs of moral goodness or lack thereof. Rich? Good for you. Poor? Get to work. No longer do we need to feel bad about these inequalities. On the contrary, we should feel good about them. For example, I once had a teacher in Sunday School claim that the same kinds of inequalities that exist in this world will continue to exist in the next life in heaven. I objected that the scriptures are fairly clear that inequalities are deeply evil and that "if ye are not equal in earthly things ye cannot be equal in obtaining heavenly things" (D&C 78:6). The teacher countered by claiming that inequalities are a result of different levels of work and that it would be immoral if we weren't unequal based on our different levels of work.

My point in bringing up this example is that for this teacher, inequality was the natural and ethical result of different levels of work—so much so that he assumed heaven would also be deeply unequal. He took this to be an obvious moral truth and struggled to understand how it could not be the case. When I pointed out a few scriptures that suggest God condemns inequality, he was genuinely perplexed and disturbed, but waved the issue away, insisting we move on.

---

3. Sandel, 121.
4. Sandel, 122.

By calling out his claim about inequality, I was threatening his entire moral order and his own sense of moral goodness. Here we see again how work and one's moral identity as a good person become intertwined:

> Much of the appeal of the meritocratic faith consists in the idea that our success is our own doing, at least under the right conditions. Insofar as the economy is a field of fair competition, untainted by privilege or prejudice, we are responsible for our fate. We succeed or fail based on our merits. We get what we deserve.
>
> This is a liberating picture, for it suggests we can be self-made human agents, the authors of our fate, the masters of our destiny. It is also morally satisfying, because it suggests the economy can answer to the ancient notion of justice as giving people their due. . . .
>
> The meritocratic emphasis on effort and hard work seeks to vindicate the idea that, under the right conditions, we are responsible for our success and thus capable of freedom. It also seeks to vindicate the faith that, if the competition is truly fair, success will align with virtue; those who work hard and play by the rules will earn the rewards they deserve.
>
> We want to believe that success, in sports and in life, is something we earn, not something we inherit.[5]

Meritocracy produces a powerful and seductive image of a just social order. Despite widespread political agreement that such a society would be desirable, Sandel argues it is not. It would create a fundamentally divided society, and he thinks these divisions would tend towards smugness and feelings of superiority in the wealthy and a deep sense of failure and resentment on the part of the poor. Of course, the situation is far worse if we have the ideological vision and a moral imaginary shaped by meritocracy in a world that is not truly meritocratic. This creates a terrible reality in which the rich are often that way through means that do not reflect hard nor, as I will be arguing, honest work, and the working poor who, try as they might, remain stuck in poverty despite their best efforts. The result is unmerited and crude hubris on the part of the wealthy and unmerited and traumatic shame for the poor.

As I conclude in *Meritocracy Mingled with Scripture*,

> A culture that recognizes the role of luck and the reality of differences in natural talents is far less likely to produce hubris in winners and humiliation in losers. Instead of bragging about how hard they work, winners might express gratitude for the talents they have been gifted and the luck that helped them. Historically, such sentiment was often articulated in terms of grace—being blessed by the gods/God or fortune. And if indeed my successes are the result

5. Sandel, 123–25.

not only of hard work, but of luck and grace, then I should be far more careful hoarding the rewards of such successes for myself. This kind of ingratitude and selfishness will likely only anger the gods and turn them against me.

If Sandel is correct, we could say that meritocratic ideals tend towards gracelessness and hubris, while inflicting humiliation on much of the population. This would be true for fully meritocratic societies but also for any society pretending to meritocracy like our own. In fact, societies that are not meritocratic, but mistakenly think they are and/or judge each other on meritocratic grounds are doubly cruel and doubly duplicitous. The poor do not have a fair chance but are blamed as if they do, and the wealthy have compounding unfair privileges but act like they don't and feel justified in their supposed superiority. Furthermore, since the meritocratic order benefits them and makes them feel morally good, they have a vested interest in not questioning or challenging it. Those who have not succeeded are more likely to see the problems with the meritocratic order, but any complaints and objections, no matter how legitimate, are likely to be ignored by those in power. The less successful may know very well how deeply unjust the meritocratic world is but have no voice and no recourse in many contexts. Just work harder, they are told.

If Sandel is correct, the ideal of meritocracy is impossible, undesirable, inhuman, promotes thoughtlessness, and is altogether deeply damaging.[6]

Honest Work

I can think of few instances where there is a starker mismatch between a widespread way of thinking and understanding what is happening in the world and what is actually happening in the world. In other words, whether or not the ideal of meritocracy is as flawed as Michael J. Sandel argues, the reality on the ground is nothing like a meritocracy. This is a testament to the power of the ideal of meritocracy—people desperately *want* it to be true and are performing stunning mental gymnastics to delude themselves that it is.

To draw out this contrast, I want to approach it through an immanent critique. What philosophers mean by "immanent critique" is an approach that accepts a particular framework and then examines how it lives up to its own standards. For example, suppose you have a Christian and a Buddhist, and the Christian is critiquing the Buddhist, but is using Christian moral standards to do so. This is a "transcendent critique," using standards from one tradition to judge another from outside it. In response, the Buddhist may simply point out that they do not accept those particular moral standards and that in Buddhism there is a different perspective.

6. Justin Pack, *Meritocracy Mingled with Scripture*, 29–30.

On the other hand, an immanent critique seeks to work within a tradition and critique it based on its own standards: if meritocracy says work is so important, let's accept this and look at work. As we've seen so far, the meritocratic ideal is that success should follow from hard work. That is, we should achieve our success, and only when we put the work in are the results truly ours. And when the results are truly ours, others do not have the right to demand we share it with them; they need to put the work in too.

What I would like to suggest is that the basic understanding of work is proportional. It is assumed that a certain amount of work has a certain value and deserves a certain reward. It is not deemed fair if two people are getting paid the same for doing roughly the same kind of work, but one works for eight hours and the other only works for two. (This is why the parable of the workers in the vineyard is a hard pill to swallow from a meritocratic perspective.) If you work more, you should get paid more.

However, here is the rub: you don't get wealthy doing proportional labor. The key to getting wealthy is precisely to break proportionality—to get paid (much) more for what one does than merely the labor involved. And this is primarily enabled by the weirdness of money.

We can see this problem better if we look not just at "hard" work, but also "honest" work. "Honest" work is a phrase often invoked by blue-collar workers: "It may not pay a lot, but it is *honest* work." What does someone mean when they claim a job is honest work? Typically, they mean that it is a job that involves physical labor, that there is a clear connection between the labor done and the product of the labor, or that the pay is intelligibly proportional to the work. Construction work is honest work. Farm work is honest work.

Based on the phrase "honest work," the foil to it would seem to be "dishonest" work, but that doesn't quite capture the opposite of "honest work." Honest work makes sense. We can see the labor being done, the product of the labor, and that pay is comprehensively proportional to the work. The opposite of this is work that doesn't make sense, often because there is no real "work" involved (like profiting from investments), the pay doesn't match the work, or the kind of work done is bullshit. It isn't real roll-up-your-sleeves work, and it isn't honest. From the perspective of honest work, bullshit work looks like taking advantage of esoteric bureaucratic or irrational monetary systems.

Let me offer an example of each. First is an example of esoteric bureaucratic work (which is often associated with "government jobs," but, in this case, is from a private company) from David Graeber:

> Kurt works for a subcontractor for the German military. Or . . . actually, he is employed by a subcontractor of a subcontractor of a subcontractor for the German military.
>
> Here is how he describes his work:
>
> The German military has a subcontractor that does their IT work.
>
> The IT firm has a subcontractor that does their logistics.
>
> The logistics firm has a subcontractor that does their personnel management, and I work for that company.
>
> Let's say soldier A moves to an office two rooms farther down the hall. Instead of just carrying his computer over there, he has to fill out a form.
>
> The IT subcontractor will get the form, people will read it and approve it, and forward it to the logistics firm.
>
> The logistics firm will then have to approve the moving down the hall, and will request personnel from us.
>
> The office people in my company will then do whatever they do, and now I come in.
>
> I get an email: "Be at barracks B at time C." Usually these barracks are one hundred to five hundred kilometers [62–310 miles] away from my home, so I will get a rental car. I take the rental car, drive to the barracks, let dispatch know that I arrived, fill out a form, unhook the computer, load the computer into a box, seal the box, have a guy from the logistics firm carry the box to the next room, where I unseal the box, fill out another form, hook up the computer, call dispatch to tell them how long I took, get a couple of signatures, take my rental car back home, send dispatch a letter with all of the paperwork and then get paid.
>
> So instead of the soldier carrying his computer for five meters, two people drive for a combined six to ten hours, fill out around fifteen pages of paperwork, and waste a good four hundred euros of taxpayers' money.[7]

The traditional foil to hard-working blue-collar jobs are "pencil pushing" white-collar jobs like this—so denigrated because they involve endless paperwork. The resentment against these jobs is not just at their much-lampooned bureaucratic absurdity, but that they often pay more than blue-collar jobs. Furthermore, not only are these jobs famous for the perceived unnecessary paperwork and their disproportionally high wages, but also for the common necessity to pretend to care about the work. The requirement is also very common in service jobs.[8] This form of BS—acting like one cares about what one is doing when one doesn't, or that one knows what one is doing when one doesn't—is perhaps the closest BS-ing comes to being dishonest, although with a connotation of not just lying

7. David Graeber, *Bullshit Jobs: A Theory*, 1–2.

8. Arlie Hochschild, *The Managed Heart: Commercialization of Human Feeling*.

or misleading but hiding what one truly feels in a way that often entails selling oneself out or not being true to oneself.

So, while the foil to "honest work" could be called "dishonest work" in more than one way, it would probably be better to call it "bullshit work." It is bullshit work not just because of the BS tasks one has to do and the BS of disproportionate pay, but also the BS-ing one has to do to appease the bosses.

Of course, finance and investing take this a step further. I asked a friend who works in finance what she actually does on a normal day. She replied that she goes to work, opens Excel spreadsheets, and spends the rest of the day messing around with numbers. It was clear from her response that there was something absurd to her about this. I asked what all the numbers were about, and she replied that she was managing investments for wealthy people. Her job was to make rich people richer, and she got paid six figures to do so. She would not claim her job was honest work. This is not to say she was doing anything illegal or dishonest, but that it was something absurd. Even more absurd than bureaucratic paperwork, this is directly taking advantage of the weirdness of money.

A particularly good example of bullshit work related to irrational monetary systems is how the rapper Vanilla Ice accidentally got rich from investing in real estate:

> Van Winkle's biggest career break was his hit song "Ice Ice Baby" released in August 1990. The song was an instant hit and went on to become the party anthem of the 90s. "We were selling a million records a day, easy!" he told Steve-O.
>
> Unfortunately, Van Winkle's rap career nosedived after "Ice Ice Baby," but the track was successful enough to help him accumulate a large portfolio of real estate.
>
> He said he bought homes "all over the country" that he "never used." When he decided to offload his properties, Van Winkle says he was surprised by how lucrative the investments had been. "They sold really quick and I made millions for doing nothing! I didn't even change the carpet . . . and I go holy s— let's go buy a bunch more of them." [9]

Vanilla Ice lets the cat out of the bag here. He bought a bunch of houses, forgot about them, and then discovered they had increased in value in the meantime. "I made millions for doing nothing!"

If a society tolerates and institutionalizes money, then many individuals and groups will seek not only to protect themselves from the weirdness

9. Vishesh Raisinghani, "'I made millions for doing nothing!': Vanilla Ice built a real estate empire and is reportedly worth $20M now."

of money, but to take advantage of it. For example, investing in stocks is one way to try and make one's money grow *without having to do anything*. However, putting it this way says the quiet part out loud. One of my fiscally savvy friends objected to this characterization and insisted that it is not making money by doing nothing, but getting a return on smart investing. In other words, he insists, the money he makes is because of the research he does. He called me up once to tease me: "Hey, I'm sitting on a beach in Florida and I made $7,000 on the market today." If I too had done the right research, I could also be making bank (by doing nothing).

Despite his protestations that this income is a legitimate result of his "research" and "smartness," it is quite clearly taking advantage of the weird plasticity of money—buying low and selling high. He wants to look like he is working for these gains, but since there is no physical labor and really nothing but pushing a button on a computer or smartphone, the only way to pretend this isn't just something quite akin to gambling or taking advantage of a bizarre monetary system is to attribute these gains to being "smart." This is a common strategy. In her ethnography of Wall Street, Karen Ho finds that such claims of "smartness" are ubiquitous in finance and function as a justification for efforts to game the system.[10] Likewise, President Donald Trump, when accused of circumventing his taxes, claimed this indicated he was "smart."[11]

It is odd that these "smart" investors often lean heavily into the language of meritocracy, claiming that they have worked hard for what they have "earned," when it is quite obvious they are often not working in any traditional sense. But we can see why. While meritocracy makes the claim that "if you work hard, success will or should follow," it is often also taken to imply that "hard work is what merits success." "Smart" investors are circumventing the requirement of hard work and finding an alternative way to get the success. While some use the claim of being "smart" as a justification for success without hard work, others, like my fiscally savvy friend, clearly feel pressure to not be seen as a moocher or to be sucking off the labor of others. He wants to be able to also claim that he is working hard and that he deserves his success.

Just opening the discussion of honest work quickly reveals a deeply disproportional economy in which different jobs pay quite differently based on a variety of factors that are often not transparent. Of course, the overarching principle is profit. This largely disconnects the value of a

---

10. Karen Ho, *Liquidated: An Ethnography of Wall Street*.
11. Daniella Diaz, "Trump: 'I'm Smart' For Not Paying Taxes."

product from the work that goes into it. What matters is demand, and this has nothing to do with labor. The most random of things can increase dramatically in value based on the stupidest of trends. A Pokemon figurine is all the craze. Stanley water bottles are flying off the shelves. Cookies are in, cupcakes are out.

From the perspective of honest work and a proportional economy, this crazy quilt of jobs and pay is irrational and alarming. The odd thing is that some, like my fiscally savvy friend, are aware that there is something ludicrous about making $7,000 while sitting on a beach in Florida. As such, they try to justify their unmerited gains by rooting them in research or smartness. Others, like Vanilla Ice, don't seem bothered and hurry up to get more where that came from. Here, any pretension to earning it simply falls away, and the question becomes simply how to get ahead. Each of these different stances can lean into meritocracy to support their position in varying degrees of cynicism or genuineness. Initially, it seems that the more one works in an honest job, the more a commitment to meritocracy will be genuine; and the more one works in a disproportionally earning job, the more one is likely to not be committed to meritocracy, to be cynical about it ("practical" about getting ahead), or, perhaps, to indeed be committed to meritocracy but deeply deluded or ignorant about living a disproportional existence.

In fact, it does seem that there are many who take advantage of disproportionality but are not conflicted at all and genuinely do think they have earned their disproportionate advantages. They are shameless because they cannot or will not think through their advantages. When they invoke meritocracy, they are not being cynical.

More than this, my suggestion is that all wealth is the result of disproportionality. One cannot get rich working proportionally, but it seems that there are many wealthy people who defend their wealth because they genuinely believe they earned it. This kind of ignorance is very useful because if they did earn it, meritocracy teaches us, then it is theirs and they do not need to share it with the poor. It is an interesting question to consider what percentage of the rich actually genuinely believe they deserve it and what percentage invoke meritocracy cynically. My suspicion is that many, if not most, are of the former.

This means that there are glaring contradictions at the heart of wealth disparity that most do not see. Otherwise we would be less comfortable with our inequalities. This failure to see and think about what we are doing is a form of thoughtlessness.

I have argued elsewhere that money leads to thoughtlessness.[12] Here I want to go further and suggest that money leads to bullshitting. A society that embraces money will become a world of bullshit. I'll explore this claim in the next two chapters. First, I will need to establish what exactly is meant by "bullshit," which is not being used here to be provocative. On the contrary, it is a rich word that captures something deeply important about the order of money and the world we have created. Using the philosopher Hannah Arendt, I will try and give some specificity to how "bullshit" will be used. With this in place, I will attempt to show how the order of money tends to lead to a world of bullshit in Chapter 6.

---

12. Justin Pack, *Money and Thoughtlessness: A Genealogy and Defense of the Traditional Suspicions of Money and Merchants.*

5. Towards an Arendtian Theory of Bullshit

The word "bullshit" is arguably one of the richest words in the English language. It can mean "a lie," "dumb," "absurd," "demeaning," "false," or "alienating." It can mean trying to look like you know an answer on a test when you don't, engaging in senseless tasks, jumping through hoops, misleading others, and a whole host of other things.

I'm not using the word to be provocative. Scholars have used it as a technical term to describe specific phenomena. When I claim money leads to a world of bullshit, I mean this both in a narrow, technical sense and also in the broader, fully loaded sense of the term. First, let me look at the famous definition of the term offered by the philosopher Harry G. Frankfurt. While I think his definition of BS is helpful, it is also very narrow. The anthropologist David Graeber has written a book about BS jobs, but I will put off discussing his argument until the next chapter. Both of these theories of BS are powerful and have proven influential, but I think the best description of BS comes from the work of Hannah Arendt, specifically from her analysis of three figures: Rahel Varnhagen, the Nazi Adolf Eichmann, and Socrates. Arendt uses the character study of the Jewish saloon mistress Rahel Varnhagen to discuss the tensions faced by an outsider to "fit in" with a society deeply prejudiced against her. Varnhagen performatively BS-es her way into German high society. Eichmann, on the other hand, was in a position of power but claimed he was just a cog in the machine and that the responsibility for what he did belonged to his bosses since he was just following orders. Arendt argues that his willingness to empty himself out to become a good soldier represents a kind of terrible moral capitulation that we find not just in Eichmann but in many people in modern society.

While both Varnhagen and Eichmann sold their souls through their BS-ing, Socrates represents, for Arendt, a refusal to BS and holding onto his integrity. In her account, he emerges as a kind of anti-BSer, someone who refuses to sell himself out to succeed in the system—a heroic example for us in modern times, caught up in bureaucratic and capitalistic systems that repeatedly require we sacrifice ourselves and our integrity to accumulation and efficiency.

In addition to this attention to moral character, Arendt connects these issues to thinking and thoughtlessness. Here the primary foil is between Eichmann as a thoughtless individual and Socrates as a thoughtful individual. But what Arendt shows is that one can think in one way, while not thinking in another. She will argue that this has become one of the primary characteristics of our times: our ability to cognize (to problem-solve), but our common failure to think. The Arendtian account allows us to see bullshit as an ethical problem that relates to the kind of people and society we are, and the kind of thinking and thoughtlessness that pervades modern life.

Frankfurt on Bullshit

Thirty years ago, Henry G. Frankfurt wrote a famous essay that was later turned into the short book *On Bullshit.* Frankfurt's claim is straightforward and insightful.[1] He argues there is a difference between lying and bullshitting: a lie hides the truth, but in so doing it recognizes the truth; bullshit, on the other hand, is indifferent to the truth—the bullshitter says whatever is useful without caring whether it is true or false. Thus, a student may BS their way through an assignment or a class discussion by trying to look like they know what they're talking about rather than making an effort to understand. What matters is not what is true; persuading others or getting the desired grade becomes what is important.

For Frankfurt, truth is foundational for civilization.[2] As such, on his account, bullshit is particularly insidious because of its lack of commitment to the truth. The liar is dangerous, but for a lie to function the liar needs most people to be committed to the truth—the lie only works if people think it is truth. The bullshitter, on the other hand, doesn't care about either the truth or lies, they just want to get the results they want. BS, then, undermines the entire register of truth and just focuses on results regardless of truth or falsity.

Using this definition, probably the best example of a bullshitter is Donald Trump. Many scholars and political observers, including Harry G. Frankfurt himself, have pointed out that Trump is a bullshit artist.[3] It is precisely the possibility of making wild assertions with little reference to reality that political observers have noticed with Trump. Anything that he doesn't like is "fake news"; and when his claims seem to fly in the face of facts, they are "alternative facts." He bullshits with little regard for truth and lies whenever it is convenient. Trump expects his enablers to make his

1. Harry G. Frankfurt, *On Bullshit.*

2. Princeton University Press, "On Bullshit Part 1."

3. Harry G. Frankfurt, "Donald Trump Is BS, Says Expert in BS"; Lauren Griffin, "Trump Isn't Lying, He's Bullshitting—And It's Far More Dangerous."

wild assertions true and surrounds himself with flattering yes-men that seek to do so. The result has been political chaos, confusion, and cruelty.

We might mistakenly think the problem of bullshit is a recent one because Trump waves it in our faces every day, but Frankfurt saw the phenomenon of bullshit three decades earlier. It predates Trump and will continue after him. As such, if we want to combat bullshit, we need to understand it as a social and political phenomenon. Frankfurt points us in the right direction, but for a fuller picture we should turn to Arendt.

Towards an Arendtian Theory of Bullshit

Hannah Arendt has also been recognized as increasingly important for understanding an era of "fake news" and "alternative facts."[4] The primary work scholars have used for this kind of analysis has been Arendt's 1951 *The Origins of Totalitarianism*.[5] It treats a wide range of issues such as populism, totalitarianism, fascism, and anti-Semitism and touches on issues of truth and facts in totalitarian society. I agree that this particular work is helpful, but I want to pull on a broader spectrum of her works to articulate an Arendtian account of bullshit. She never uses the word herself in her writings, but I am going to suggest that it is one of the primary concerns of her philosophy, tied to her concern with the thoughtlessness of modern society, and her longed-for bullshit-free spaces.

This is a more far-reaching set of claims than those made by Frankfurt, but I think they enrich his account and are also illuminating about the present. We can begin to understand an Arendtian theory of bullshit by looking at three figures that feature prominently in Arendt's philosophy: the BSers Rahel Varnhagen and Adolf Eichmann, and the anti-BSer Socrates.

Arendt wrote a biography of the German Jewish socialite and salon owner Rahel Varnhagen (1771–1833). This might seem quite odd, considering at first glance it appears to have very little to do with the kinds of things that Arendt was concerned with in her other works. If, however, as I am asserting, we recognize Arendt's concern with bullshit, then the philosophical importance of this text becomes more apparent. Varnhagen was a Jewish woman living in an anti-Semitic society who, in order to ingratiate her way into high society had "to master the 'art of representing her own

---

4. Zoe Williams, "Totalitarianism in the Age of Trump: Lessons from Hannah Arendt"; Sean Illing, "A 1951 Book About Totalitarianism Is Flying Off the Shelves. Here's Why."

5. Hannah Arendt, *The Origins of Totalitarianism*.

life: the point was not to tell the truth, but to display herself; not always to say the same thing to everyone, but to each what was appropriate for him.'"[6] For Arendt, this made Varnhagen a BSer and a model for Arendt of what it means to bullshit. She has to become protean, to create and manage a persona that not only hides anything Jewish—whether that be physical appearance, behavior, language, mannerisms, religious beliefs, and so forth—but also embraces the appearances, behaviors, languages, and mannerisms of various positions within German "high society." She has to manage impressions so as to fit the expectations of these social circles.

This tightrope act of being caught between different cultures and identities is one that has been described as existing in a liminal state, in what Gloria Anzaldùa calls the "borderlands," with all the tensions of attempting to navigate differing, contradictory, often harmful expectations.[7] Anzaldùa describes herself as being caught between patriarchal, homophobic Latino culture and racist, patriarchal, homophobic North American culture. Many Jews in Europe were stuck in a similar situation. Arendt uses the language of Bernard Lazare to show how the Jewish outsider had two options: to be the pariah or the parvenu.[8] The pariah can hold on to her traditions but will remain an outcast. The parvenu, on the other hand, must cast aside her traditions and seek to assimilate. This is not a simple task. Even if she can manage to come across as "like everyone else," she may often be treated as "the Jew that doesn't act like a Jew and acts like us." [9]

The kind of bullshit that Arendt is describing here is not quite the same as what Frankfurt describes. It involves not an indifference to truth, but a (often disingenuous) performance of certain expected social norms or duties despite their arbitrariness or absurdity. One is faced with the requirement to perform in certain ways that differ from how one would otherwise act. It is apparent to the outsider that this required role is arbitrary, and it may seem completely absurd. In fact, their recognition of this absurdity is precisely because their outsider status allows them to see it as one way of being or acting among others. Bullshitting in this case then is when one sucks it up and completes or plays along with absurd and arbitrary requirements in order to get some desired results.

---

6. Hannah Fenichel Pitkin, *The Attack of the Blob: Hannah Arendt's Concept of the Social*, 26.

7. Gloria Anzaldúa, *Borderlands/La Frontera: The New Mestiza.*

8. Pitkin, *The Attack of the Blob*, 21.

9. Pitkin, 21.

In such situations we hear phases like: "Ugh, I am going to BS my way through this" or "I have to put up with so much BS at my job." If we accept that there is some kind of truth to identity ("I am Jewish") or an authentic self ("I am an artist"), then hiding or setting aside this true identity or authentic self is a kind of selling oneself out. However, there doesn't have to be a settled truth about identity or self to experience being forced to jump through hoops, play the part, or sell oneself. Thus, bullshit here does not have to be a matter of truth like Frankfurt describes; it may simply be a matter of doing or putting up with bullshit requirements. A world of bullshit is a world in which everyone has to act and talk in certain ways, manage impressions, and perform tasks they think are stupid, and we do it because "you gotta do what you gotta do."

It has not been lost on Arendt scholars that Arendt herself was a German Jewish woman in an anti-Semitic society and that the tensions she describes for Rahel Varnhagen were tensions Arendt herself experienced.[10] But these are not just tensions for the outsider. For Arendt the modern world demands we all assimilate ourselves into the giant economic family that she later calls "the social." In her *On Revolution*, she characterizes modernity as having "degenerated into mere administration, the public realm has vanished; there is no space either for seeing or being seen in action. . . . [P]olitical matters are . . . dictated by necessity to be decided by experts, but not open to opinions and genuine choice."[11] The position of the parvenu is particularly perilous, but in a certain sense modern society demands everyone mold themselves into a functional part of the modern machine.

This brings us to the second example of a BSer: the Nazi Adolf Eichmann.

During World War II, Eichmann had overseen the organization of Jews to be sent to the concentration camps. He proved himself highly competent as a logistical orchestrator of the Holocaust. After the war Eichmann fled to Argentina where he was eventually discovered and taken to Israel to be put on trial. Arendt was asked to attend the trial and report on it for the *Atlantic Monthly* magazine.

According to Arendt, the prosecutors tried to paint Eichmann as a hateful monster, which is how we tend to imagine Nazis.[12] However, Eichmann presented himself very much like Max Weber's description

---

10. Norma Moruzzi, "From Parvenu to Pariah: Hannah Arendt's *Rahel Varnhagen*."

11. Hannah Arendt, *On Revolution*, 237.

12. Hannah Arendt, *Eichmann in Jerusalem*.

of the honorable civil servant—a dedicated cog dutifully following the orders of those higher up in the machine. He even claimed to not be anti-Semitic. As a trapped bureaucrat following the orders of his bosses, he should not be blamed, after all, if he was just doing his job. If he hadn't done it, someone else would have.[13]

Eichmann is the extreme result of BS-ing. Unlike Varnhagen, whom Arendt presents as having a certain ethnic identity that she hides and sells out, Eichmann is presented as so empty that he is the ultimate protean yes-man. Arendt says "every line of [his notes made in jail] shows his utter ignorance of everything that was not directly, technically, and bureaucratically connected with his job."[14] He was good at his job, turning the killing of Jews into an "assembly line."[15] He committed everything to his job and internalized the supercilious catchphrases and slogans of his time.[16] This all came together to create an insulated, career-obsessed, and highly motivated bureaucrat. Eichmann has sold himself out to the machine so thoroughly that he seems to be empty, so devoid of integrity and conscience that he is willing to sacrifice others to the machine. His emptiness and insulation safeguard him from "the presence of others, and hence reality as such."[17]

Eichmann's defense that he was just a cog in the machine feels particularly grotesque and shocking in the context of the Nazi concentration camps, and not surprisingly it was hard for many to take Eichmann's defense seriously. But Arendt argued that this kind of vapid moral thoughtlessness combined with logistical competence was not an aberration; it was something she seemed to see everywhere. She saw it in the failure of Adenhauer and the German government to deal with returning Nazi soldiers appropriately. Instead of working through what they had done, Arendt believed Germans were too quick to just try to get back to normal. She saw it, most controversially, in Jewish councils that provided information to Nazis. And she saw it in her adoptive country of America. In

---

13. It is worth noting that there is now strong evidence that Eichmann was performing being an innocent cog in the machine, and that in reality he was just as much a wretched Nazi racist as many expected. As Susan Neiman claims, this doesn't undermine Arendt's analysis of thoughtlessness, however, since she sees it in many people, not just Eichmann. See the afterword in Susan Neiman, *Evil in Modern Thought: An Alternative History of Philosophy*.

14. Arendt, *Eichmann in Jerusalem*, 54.

15. Arendt, 45.

16. Arendt, 42, 48.

17. Arendt, 49.

The Human Condition, Arendt claims that thoughtlessness "seems to me among the outstanding characteristics of our time."[18]

We can give her claim more specificity by using the terminology she introduced in her last book, *The Life of the Mind*. In it, she distinguishes between at least three different kinds of thinking: cognition, wonder, and contemplation. By cognition, Arendt means what we would now call "problem-solving." By wonder, Arendt means being lost in thought and Socratic curiosity. By contemplation, she means meditating and bringing oneself close to a work of art, the cosmos, God, and so on.[19] Cognition is a kind of thinking that is highly useful and productive. It gets results. As such, it is highly valued in modern society. Wonder and contemplation are much less useful and are therefore discouraged in modern education. But, according to Arendt, wonder is particularly important. While wonder tends to come to no conclusions, provides no answers, and is therefore ostensibly useless, critically it has the potential unintended effect of causing us to think about alternatives and to question the status quo. Wonder is so important for Arendt that she tends to, confusingly, just refer to it as thinking. Cognition, while more encouraged and more common in modern life, gets a separate term that distinguishes it from thinking or as a different type of thinking. When Arendt worries about the lack of thinking in modern society, she means the lack of thinking as wonder. There is plenty of cognition going on.

Thoughtlessness in modern society for Arendt is most often wonderless cognition. It is problem-solving that doesn't stop to wonder about the implications of the solutions it offers. Our thoughtless society is not one in which people are not using their brains. They are, but they are using them to solve problems. Unfortunately, Arendt thinks, we aren't taking the time to wonder in a way that may cause us to question the status quo—in this context, the hegemony of problem-solving. Victor Frankenstein is making his monster without thinking enough about whether he should. We are making Jurassic Park without enough thought to whether we should. We have radically changed our lives in many ways without thinking enough about what exactly that means for the human condition. To be clear, thinking as wonder is not a purposeful process that always questions the status quo; it can be more of a meandering that often wanders off the trail and, as a result, is more likely to cause us to wonder about the trail.

---

18. Hannah Arendt, *The Human Condition*, 5.

19. For a fuller elaboration see Justin Pack, "The Need for a Phenomenology of Academic Activity under Neoliberalism."

Cognition, on the other hand, tends to stick to the trails and seek to accomplish established goals.

Eichmann was good at solving problems but bad at wondering in a way that might have raised doubt about the moral failings of what he was doing. So too, modern society is constantly accelerating forward with new inventions, new innovations, and new technological powers, but is too rarely thinking enough about what we are doing. For Arendt, we are far too confident in our abilities, and due to this thoughtlessness we are endangering our worlds.[20]

Arendt's analysis allows us to see how we can think in one way (cognition) but not think in others (wonder). This thoughtless cognition is particularly dangerous because by mistaking cognition for thinking, we tend to think we are being thoughtful and careful when we are not. This can result in the kinds of odd and crude internal contradictions I brought up in the last section. The result is cultural practices that are taken for granted despite sometimes having terrible flaws. When she says Eichmann is thoughtless, she means he can solve problems but fails to wonder or question what he is doing and why. He is doing bullshit tasks, but he seemingly does so without the conflict and frustration that normally accompany such things.

Frankfurt says bullshit is indifferent to truth; Arendt's Eichmann seems to have become an empty vessel that mindlessly accepts the "truths" he has been filled with. Eichmann is not indifferent to the truth; he is unwilling or incapable of thinking about whether what he has been taught is correct. The dynamic here is one that we see commonly criticized in pop culture: the mindless cog-in-the-machine office worker that does BS tasks without any seeming internal resistance; the teacher's pet that does whatever they are asked; the political yes-man and the obsequious businessman, enthusiastic for the next banal task that will help them move up the ladder. There is a similarity to Frankfurt's BSer here as we find a kind of indifference to the absurdity or immorality of whatever task is required. The results are all that matters. We could call this the "banality of bullshit." There is a clear connection here between bullshit, thoughtlessness, and the banality of evil.

To better understand the connection between bullshit and thoughtlessness, we need to turn to Socrates, whom Arendt presents as a foil to Eichmann and Varnhagen.

---

20. This claim is explored in Justin Pack, *Amor Mundi and Overcoming Modern World Alienation.*

The Anti-BS Socrates

Socrates won't bullshit and won't put up with bullshit. During his trial he not only calls out Meletus for his unctuous prosecution of Socrates on trumped-up, bullshit charges but also, instead of shutting up and doing what he is told like a good lackey, famously lambasts the citizens of Athens for being obsessed with money, honor, and fame instead of caring about wisdom, truth, and their own souls. When given the chance to wiggle out the back door, he drinks the hemlock poison. Arendt, like many philosophers before her, sees Socrates as a figure of integrity. Integrity is perhaps the opposite of bullshitting.

A key part of Socrates's integrity is not turning off or ignoring his wonder and questions. Children are always asking questions and do not seem to know when to stop. However, thinking as just wonder is inefficient. It rarely finds answers (much like Socrates in Plato's dialogues). In contemporary consumer society, as we go through school and later get jobs, we are discouraged from wondering, being lost in thought, and questioning. Instead we are encouraged to be useful, get stuff done, and calculate the most efficient results. In Arendtian terms we are discouraged from thinking and encouraged to cognize. The problem, however, is that cognition can be thoughtless. We can participate in projects that have far-reaching consequences without wanting or bothering to think about these consequences. We just want to get that paycheck. We may perform tasks for a job that we would prefer not to, or even worse, that we might find immoral. These tasks may demand a high level of cognition while discouraging thinking.

Arendt suggests that thinking may be related to the development of a conscience, that voice in our head that questions what we are doing and makes us think twice. Socrates again features prominently in her analysis. Because he allows himself to think and question, Socrates constantly engages in dialogue with others. They have perspectives that might illuminate his questions. Once one has been exposed to different perspectives, it becomes possible to voice them to oneself, to carry on a conversation with oneself. This can result in what Arendt calls the "2-in-1"—having another voice in your head, or a conscience that questions and challenges.[21] Thus, Socrates says he is never alone and that when he goes home there is a person waiting for him. This is his conscience, a version of himself who will witness against him and question him. Socrates is his own gadfly.

21. Hannah Arendt, *The Life of the Mind.*

Eichmann, however, was no Socrates. Arendt claims that to end up like him in a cog in the thoughtless machine,

> all [one] has to do is never start the soundless solitary dialogue we call "thinking," never go home and examine things. This is not a matter of wickedness or goodness, as it is not a matter of intelligence or stupidity. A person who does not know that silent intercourse (in which we examine what we say and what we do) will not mind contradicting himself, and this means he will never be either willing to account for what he says or does; nor will he mind committing any crime, since he can count on its being forgotten the next moment. Bad people—Aristotle to the contrary notwithstanding—are *not* "full of regrets."[22]

I would suggest that it is not enough just to not think; it also requires being willing to bullshit. Bullshitting shuts down thinking. It excuses what it does, like Eichmann did, by saying, "If I don't do it someone else will," or "I may not like this, but one has to make a living." These kinds of self-exculpations diminish thinking and hollow a person out, potentially leaving them an empty yes-man.

Thus when Arendt claims in *The Human Condition* that thoughtlessness is "among the outstanding characteristics of our time," I want to suggest we add to this that bullshit is one of the outstanding characteristics of our time.[23] Arendt wanted to be free from this bullshit.

Arendt's Hope: Freedom from Bullshit, Bullshit-Free Spaces

In addition to being the paradigmatic anti-BSer, Hannah Arendt claims Socrates sought to establish a bullshit-free space. The claim here is that Socrates sought to change the *polis*, which was already conceived of as a space of freedom from the economic private sphere of the home, from a place of agonistic competition to a place of friendly dialogue and thinking. Socrates condemned the spiritually unhealthy obsession with money, honor, and fame, which we can imagine included all sorts of image management, flattery, aggrandizement, exaggeration, and so on, in favor of the honest dialogical search for wisdom. Arendt claims that "politically speaking, Socrates tried to make friends out of Athens's citizenry." [24] Instead of trying to competitively best each other, "they become equal partners in a common world—that they together constitute a community. Community is what friendship achieves."[25]

22. Arendt, 191.
23. Arendt, *The Human Condition*.
24. Arendt, 82.
25. Arendt, 83.

In her account, after the *polis* rejected Socrates, his most famous student, Plato, was so frustrated that he rejected both the agonistic democracy of the *polis* and Socrates's alternative of the friendly *polis* in favor of the rule of expert philosopher-kings. Western thought has followed Plato's lead, and the bullshit-free community Socrates imagined has become a forgotten alternative.[26]

Despite the adherence to the rule of experts in Western thought, Western history has seen moments of bullshit-free communities during revolutions. Without going into her full account, Arendt claims that "the ultimate end of revolution was freedom and the constitution of a public space where freedom could appear."[27] While her primary focus in *On Revolution* is the American and French revolutions, she thinks that these spontaneous spaces of people working together have appeared in many revolutions (such as the Russian revolution and the Hungarian revolution of 1956). The fact that there seems to be repeated efforts to establish public spaces of political freedom in very different settings and without "conscious imitation" of other such efforts reflects, for Arendt, the deep desire of many people for political freedom and political happiness.[28] This is not to say that everyone has such a desire; rather, it is common enough that we see the repeated spontaneous efforts in diverse times and places.[29] Unfortunately, according to Arendt these revolutionary spaces of political freedom have never received adequate institutional support and historically have always been forgotten and replaced by more efficient, less democratic institutions.

Thus there is an original rejection and forgetting of the space of political freedom and political happiness proposed by Socrates, as well as the historically repeated failure to recognize the importance of these spaces when they arise spontaneously. They have never been given the recognition and intuitional support to prevent them from disappearing again. In an indication of how important it is for her, Arendt calls this political freedom "lost treasure." She uses this phrase in various places, and while I cannot say for sure, I suspect she pulls it from a remarkable description of these free political spaces from a French resistance fighter in the Second World War, René Char:

---

26. Justin Pack, "Arendt's Genealogy of Thinking."
27. Arendt, *On Revolution*, 255.
28. Arendt, 256.
29. Arendt, 280.

> His book of aphorisms was written during the last year of the war in a frankly apprehensive anticipation of liberation; for he knew that as far as they were concerned there would be not only the welcome liberation from German occupation but liberation from the "burden" of public business as well. Back they would have to go to the épisseur *triste* of their private lives and pursuits, to the "sterile depression" of the pre-war years, when it was as though a curse hung over everything they did: "if I survive, I know that I shall have to break with the aroma of these essential years, silently reject (not repress) my treasure." The treasure, he thought, was that he had "*found* himself," that he no longer suspected himself of "insincerity," that he needed no mask and no make-believe to appear, that wherever he went he appeared as he was to others and to himself, that he could afford "to go naked." These reflections are significant enough as they testify to the involuntary self-discourse, to the joys of appearing in word and deed without equivocation and without self-reflection that are inherent in action.[30]

Char had experienced a brief period during the war free from BS, in which he did not have to constantly think about his appearance to his bosses and his peers. He was able to "go naked"—to say what he really thought, to be honest, and to be true to others and to himself.

This quote not only ends *On Revolution*, it also begins the preface to the compilation of essays included in Arendt's *Between Past and Future*.[31] It shows the central importance for Arendt of freedom from "insincerity," from "masks," and from "make-believe" that are demanded by highly administered, image-obsessed modernity (whether fascist, communist, or capitalist).

While we don't have to accept all the different aspects of Arendt's philosophy to see the value of her theory of bullshit, I have presented some of these details to attempt to show how bullshit connects many facets of her thought. Bullshit is closely related to thoughtlessness, and the willingness to bullshit may be connected to the kind of thoughtlessness we find in figures like Eichmann. Bullshitting is demanded by the machinery of modern consumer society, and each of us now faces the decision of to what degree we will allow ourselves to be sucked into "the social." Like Socrates, Rahel Varnhagen, and Adolf Eichmann, we all face decisions about what we are willing to do or not do in order to be "successful." Bullshitting, then, is also connected to consumerism: the more we allow ourselves to be consumed, the more we have to bullshit and put up with it. The more we do so, the more it will seem natural. Ours is very much a world of bullshit.

---

30. Arendt, 280.

31. Hannah Arendt, *Between Past and Future.*

Arendt's theory of bullshit enriches Frankfurt's by taking it beyond the register of truth and examining it in a sociopolitical context. Arendt sees bullshit as a phenomenon that has increased in modernity with the rise of "the social" and helps us to understand the absurdity of the bullshit we have to put up with and the bullshit we are expected to do. To bullshit or not to bullshit is an existential and ethical choice we must make every day.

The Commercialization of Emotional Labor

To finish this chapter, I want to give some practical examples of Arendtian BS to help make her theory more concrete. To begin with, let's look at a humorous exchange between David Mitchell and Stephen Frye that illustrates the problem of BS:

> David Mitchell: The thing that seems unfair to me is the number of people who are expected to pretend they care about jobs they don't care about. You should be allowed to say, look I'm fulfilling my contract. You can't put in the contract, also you have to seem like you give a shit. I think that is expecting too much. That's why I really like the fact we live in a country with such poor customer service [Britain]. I've got respect for that. This is a horrible train, you're tearing tickets, of course you're in an awful mood.
>
> Stephen Frye: Now that you put it like that, I should feel better about it. You're right. Why have a cheesy grin on your face, if you are working in an awful supermarket?
>
> David Mitchell: It's the sign either of a liar or a moron.[32]

Mitchell's humorous complaint points right at the phenomenon of BS—the need to hide what one really thinks and feels to fit the expectations of a particular situation. He and Stephen Frye are discussing this in the context of consumer capitalism, specifically in service industries. While many work settings in modern life require BS-ing to a boss or a teacher of some sort, service jobs are particularly illustrative because they also require BS-ing to customers.

One of the great analyses of the exploitation of emotional labor that occurs in the service industry is Arlie Hochschild's *The Managed Heart*. The theoretical background for her study is Ervin Goffman's dramaturgical approach. Goffman analyzed social interactions in terms of a theatrical metaphor, speaking of the preparations we make "backstage" and our "performance" when we are "on stage." Hochschild applied this theatrical lens to look at how flight attendants are required to "perform" in certain ways that require often intense forms of emotional labor.

---

32. The8431123, "David Mitchell - Customer Service Rant."

Hochschild builds on Rousseau's argument that "personality" is "becoming a form of capital" to claim that "[w]hat was once a private act of emotion management is sold now as labor in public-contact jobs."[33] In other words, "[i]t is not simply individuals who manage their feelings in order to do a job; whole organizations have entered the game."[34] The Delta airline attendants she studies are hired not only to provide in-flight snacks and drinks; they are also supposed to create a safe and happy environment. While many jobs pay for the use of the body, physical labor, and the mind (mental labor), jobs in the service industry also demand emotional labor:

> It does not take capitalism to turn feeling into a commodity or to turn our capacity for managing feeling into an instrument. But capitalism has found a use for emotion management, and so it has organized it more efficiently and pushed it further. And perhaps it does take a capitalist sort of incentive system to connect emotional labor to competition and to go so far as to actually advertise a "sincere" smile. Train workers to produce such a smile, supervise their production of it, and then forge a link between this activity and corporate profit.[35]

It is not just flight attendants that are expected to perform emotional labor. Hochschild also gives the interesting example of debt collectors. Unlike the labor of being comforting required of flight attendants, debt collectors need to act suspicious and mean. This conveys to debtors that the collectors and the companies paying them are serious and will deliver on the promise of punishments if not complied with. These examples are similar to the example I have already given of the used car salesman that acts like a friend in order to try and make a sale. This too involves emotional management.

Hochschild distinguishes between "deep" and "surface" acting in emotional labor.[36] Surface acting is when you might feel one way, say angry, but present in another way, say happy. Hochschild, however, argues that the flight attendants at Delta were taught and encouraged to not only present as happy, but to try and genuinely be happy. The result of this kind of deep acting is that one doesn't actually need to pretend; one actually becomes what one is seeking to be.

---

33. Arlie Russell Hochschild, *The Managed Heart: Commercialization of Human Feeling*, 185–86.

34. Hochschild, 185.

35. Hochschild, 186.

36. Hochschild, 33.

One of the problems that should be apparent here is the question of who and what a person is when they are wearing masks on the surface and at a deep level. The reason Delta encourages the flight attendants to engage in deep acting is, among other things, that the facade of a surface emotion can slip. Getting more commitment from their workers helps combat cynicism about the emotional atmosphere that is being created. However, deep acting raises questions about selfhood and authenticity. Is there a "real" me? If I am constantly acting or deep acting, am I harming my authentic self? Questions of authenticity and identity are quite complex, and Arendt, without using the term, clearly worries that constantly submitting to BS requirements—and it would seem especially to ones that involve misshaping the self—destroys the conscience. If I am required to be protean and constantly warp myself into something other than what I am or how I genuinely feel, I run the risk of losing that "core" of self-identity. There ends up being little left that can resist when given directions.

The kind of masks that we are asked to wear are often gendered. Hochschild sees Christopher Lasch's description of the narcissist type as an image men often emulate. The narcissist seeks attention and admiration in "a Hobbesian dog-eat-dog world."[37] While her focus on flight attendants and service work leads her to analyze primarily the kind of masks that are worn there, one of the virtues of her approach is that she clearly recognizes that the competitive world of ladder-climbing and "winning" requires masks too. One has to act tough, aggressive, calculative, strategic, and stoic—and put on the corresponding masks. But this structures the social world as a place of competition for diminishing returns. Since everyone is posturing and strutting about, there is an empty falseness to victories—respect is not genuine but begrudging, admiration is not genuine but faked. Other scholars following Hochschild have further examined different masculinities and the masks involved.[38] Hochschild focus is primarily on women, and she notices a different type:

> But our culture has produced another form of false self: the altruist, the person who is overly concerned with the needs of others. In our culture, women—because they have traditionally been assigned the task of tending to the needs of others—are in great danger of overdeveloping the false self and losing track of its boundaries. If developing a narcissistic fake self is the greater danger for men, developing an altruistic false self is the greater danger for women. Whereas the narcissist is adept at turning the social uses of feeling to his own

37. Hochschild, 195.

38. Generally considered the classic work in this regard is R. W. Connel, *Masculinities.*

> advantage, the altruist is more susceptible to being used—not because her sense of self is weaker but because her "true self" is bonded more securely to the group and its welfare.[39]

It should be pointed out that even though this analysis is now forty years old, women still tend to heavily dominate careers that are associated with emotional labor and care work (public education, nursing, childcare, and so on), although Hochschild has argued traditionally "female" arenas of "intimate life" have been increasingly commercialized, and women working in service and non-service positions are often being required to act more like the traditionally "male" narcissist.[40]

It is also important to recognize that no individual has only one "social role." Gloria Anzaldùa, who I introduced briefly earlier, has given a striking account of the tensions she experiences as a lesbian Latina woman born in Texas in a community that predates the United States.[41] Even though she was born in the US, because she was raised in an impoverished Latino community near the border of Mexico, she and others like her were often subject to racism and treated as if they were not "American" by whites. At the same time, she was not considered fully Mexican by Mexicans because she was not raised in Mexico. Furthermore, she was subject to sexism and homophobia from both cultures. Anzaldùa's account is less about the masks she had to wear at different times to fit into different settings (although there are many accounts from other authors that deal with dynamics like this) than how she was subject to cruel treatment from multiple cultures. Her experience shows the ways social and cultural pressures are multiple and layered. Indeed, all human experience happens in a complex nexus of multiple layers of meaning and morality, and attempting to understand these experiences requires an intersectional approach that tracks these many different tensions.

The reason for turning to Hochschild and Anzaldùa briefly here is to offer a practical example of how we each face, every day, a complex set of demands about how we will "perform" our race, gender, sexual orientation, job, roles, religion, and so forth. Often we do so unconsciously through habituated behavior, and so we don't think about or recognize that we are doing so. If and when we have to step outside of our typical routines, the way we are performing social expectations may become more apparent,

---

39. Hochschild, *The Managed Heart*, 195–96.

40. Arlie Russell Hochschild, *The Commercialization of Intimate Life: Notes from Home and Work*.

41. Anzaldúa, *Borderlands/La Frontera*.

and we may have to make specific decisions about how we will act. For someone like Anzaldùa who is constantly subject to discriminatory social expectations, these tensions may be far more apparent. For someone like myself, a white male raised in a society that privileges white men, these pressures may be less. Traveling to other cultures often results in shifts in what is "normal," which can cause us to see and have to make decisions about these tensions. The fact that some individuals, especially individuals in "deviant" or marginalized groups, are more likely to see these dynamics and be able to name the injustices involved gives them what scholars have called "epistemic privilege"—simply put, due to their "outsider" position, they will tend to see what is happening in this regard more clearly.

To be clear, I am not trying to claim that conforming to social standards is always BS-ing. Rather, I'm trying to use the tensions involved in taking up a role to help illustrate how we can compromise our integrity in this process. I also don't want to claim this is the only way to BS. Hopefully, what Arendt's analysis does is give us examples of BS-ing and anti-BS-ing that help better orient ourselves toward the phenomenon of BS-ing.

In the next chapter, I will show how the order of money creates a world of BS. This, of course, increases the need to compromise our integrity to achieve financial success.

6. A World of BS

The ideal of meritocracy requires a proportional economy. If the amount of money one gains as a result of work is disproportionately high, then one can't really claim to have earned it.[1] This is even more true in the case of passive income, speculative finance, crime, and so on. In these cases, one hasn't earned money but gamed the system.

The problem is that modern inequality is justified by meritocracy, so these unjustifiably disproportionate gains must pretend to be meritocratic. Thus, we get alternative explanations like the claims that being "smart" or doing "research" justify speculative gains. These sorts of claims are nonsense, but they seem to be accepted.

These critical contradictions are widely ignored because meritocracy is not just a political system, but also a moral one that shapes self and social identity. If wealth is (mis)taken to be a sign of hard work, and hard work is taken as a sign of moral goodness, then wealth is (mis)taken as a sign of moral goodness: "I worked hard for this. I am a good person. I deserve this." While there are some, like Vanilla Ice, that do not seem to care whether what they are doing is moral or not, many want the affirmation of their moral goodness as much as, or perhaps more than, they want the wealth itself. They are outraged when they are challenged on this point. It isn't just the wealthy who want to be affirmed as morally good; many who are not wealthy, especially those who actually do honest work, take comfort that they work hard ("it may not pay much but it is honest work"), and that this makes them a good person. Even many of those who are not doing well want meritocracy to be true because they want to believe their reward is coming if they work hard.

Furthermore, since wealth cannot be achieved except through disproportionate means, many of which require turning off what Hannah Arendt calls thinking (wondering about what we are doing and why) in favor of cognition (problem-solving in given scenarios), these money-driven systems not only encourage BS, but also thoughtlessness. The result is

1. In a disproportional economy one can claim one merits more because what one designed, made, or did was particularly profitable—say, if one made an exciting new invention. But in such a case, it rarely makes sense to appeal to the work involved since the amount of work is most often disproportional to the profits. And yet, the moral value is tied to work and not necessarily to profit. As such, those who have succeeded in this way often still appeal to their hard work.

an increasing inability to think about and see the contradictions that are everywhere around us.

Let me state the point frankly. From the perspective of a proportional economy, the result is horrific: the crude and cruel denigration of the poor combined with a character-destroying world of bullshit and thoughtlessness. Tellingly, when I have pointed this out in conversation the claim about the poor is often largely shrugged off (thus affirming its veracity), but the claim that a world of BS morally damages even those who are succeeding in it draws attention, because it cuts to the heart of personal and social moral identity. Efforts to succeed in our supposedly meritocratic society reflect not moral goodness, but moral self-destruction.

The horror of the world we have created is all the more striking when we consider how proud many are of it. This reflects the intense propaganda we are subjected to, our intense need to feel like we are a morally good people, and the success of the ideology of meritocracy to function as a theodicy.

In this chapter, let's look first at our hatred of the poor and then turn to our moral self-destruction through BS-ing.

Aporophobia

We treat the poor like garbage.

As Adela Cortina argues, we regularly submit the poor to hate speech and hate crimes, but we don't even realize it because we think they deserve it. Cortina gives examples of hate speech and hate crimes against the poor in Europe, where she is writing. I am writing in the United States, and there are many examples here. Perhaps the most obvious is the sustained and cruel attack upon immigrants. Despite biblical injunctions to care for the stranger and the migrant, American conservativism is riddled with racist and derisive language against migrants from Latin America. This despicable language has become so common that President Donald Trump was reelected despite, or perhaps because of, his constant hate speech against immigrants. During his first presidency, Trump and Republicans tore immigrant families apart in an effort to dissuade further immigration. These were hate crimes targeted at the poor, and now that Americans have voted him in again he has intensified his attacks on immigrants by revoking the legal resident status of thousands as he sends ICE into neighborhoods, businesses, churches, children's events, and elsewhere to traumatize families and individuals.

Cortina claims a large part of our failure to understand these crimes against immigrants as hate crimes and hate speech is that we don't have a word for abusive actions targeted at the poor. She proposes we use the term *aporophobia*, and defines it as:

> The contempt for the poor, the rejection of the person who takes but cannot give back, or at least seems unable to give back. And who, for that reason, is excluded from the world built on political, economic, and social contracts, a world of giving and receiving, in which only those who seem to have something interesting to offer in return are welcome.[2]

This contemptuous aporophobia is not limited to immigrants, but extends to the homeless, those on welfare, and even those working minimum-wage jobs. The homeless are a common target of aporophobia. It is common for governments to buy them bus tickets and send them on to the next city. As Cotina puts it,

> In an exchange based society the poor are rejected because they bring only problems to those trying to prosper, breed contempt when contemplated from a position of superiority, stoke fear when they produce insecurity, and are, at the least, tolerated with an impatience among those hoping one way or another to get rid of them.[3]

Before immigrants, one of the biggest targets was single mothers (especially Black women) who rely on state help, shamed as "welfare mothers."[4] Even those who work minimum-wage jobs are treated with disdain. The federal minimum wage hasn't increased since 2009.

There are many ways aporophobia is built into our social institutions, and indeed, in the physical world itself. I have always been struck by where and how we build our homes. In the United States, we find gated suburban communities which keep outsiders out. In some places the wealthy choose to live in communities away from city centers or up in the hills where they can have more privacy and space to build on. And those city centers also shun the poor with efforts such as equipping benches with bumps that make sleeping on them uncomfortable. In other places, the rich take up the prime real estate in attractive cities and leave the poor to crumbling neighborhoods. When I lived in Mexico, I often saw the poor relegated to hillsides or to unregulated communities that popped up on the edge of towns where there was no infrastructure. The point here is that the physical world is marred by these differences. Physical communities,

---

2. Adela Cortina, *Aporophobia: Why We Reject the Poor Instead of Helping Them*, xviii.

3. Cortina, 104–5.

4. Nancy Fraser and Linda Gordon, "A Genealogy of Dependency: Tracing a Keyword of the U.S. Welfare State."

space, density, cleanliness, pollution, infrastructure, and so on often have jarring differences based on the wealth of the communities.

Not surprisingly, the quality of the schools, the social support, the presence and kind of law enforcement, and the kinds of available food also tend to be tied to the wealth of the surrounding community. I recall visiting Santa Barbara, California, for the first time and being frustrated with the ostentatious wealth. I drove around, curious where the poorer people lived. Finally, I stopped to get lunch and talked with various locals. I asked them where the poor folk lived. They all shook their heads. There was nowhere.

Of course, with housing—like clothing—part of the point is precisely to distinguish one's wealth, and therefore one's moral goodness from others. In other words, not only are our inequalities writ large, we write them large.

Cortina offers an evolutionary explanation for aporophobia. We don't need to recount why she thinks this is the case, but she believes that we have to fight back against our at least partially natural inclination to be aporophobic. We need to educate ourselves out of these prejudices. I would suggest that whatever the case is for some evolutionary roots of aporophobia, the problem is far more social than biological. Currently we educate ourselves *into* aporophobia, or at least much deeper into it.

Here again we find ourselves at a moment where the biblical tradition is not only overwhelmingly condemnatory of inequality and wealth but also insists the justice and morality of a community be measured by the condition of the widow and the orphan. And yet, a meritocratic system that seems to embody the opposite of this has now become widely accepted.

I have always been struck by the inequality in Latter-day Saint wards and how wealth and housing inequality is almost always a taboo topic. Most have completely mixed up meritocracy with the gospel, much to our detriment. And yet, these very same meritocratic principles make it harder for many to care about the poor. The thinking is that we will help, but there is only so much we can do. Ultimately, they have to help themselves. Meanwhile, we will enjoy the large houses and wealth we have earned.

Tellingly, when I have discussed these issues with others of a meritocratic persuasion, the condition of the poor is acknowledged, but, as Cortina would predict, largely ignored. Again, their problem. But I've discovered that the topic that often does get the attention of these same individuals is the claim that the "haves" are also deeply damaged by the system, except they are damaged by the BS they must perform to succeed. This claim directly confronts the meritocratic pretension of superiority from success and inverts it—wealth isn't a sign of moral goodness; it is a sign of morally compromising oneself to inhuman, exploitative, and absurd demands. It isn't just the poor that are abused in a money-driven world of bullshit, but also the affluent.

BS Jobs

Here we can turn to David Graeber's analysis of BS jobs. Initially, Graeber wrote a short piece about how many jobs are not necessary. If they disappeared, society would keep on working.[5] And yet, not only do many of these jobs exist, but many are high paying. Not surprisingly, then, many people seek out these kinds of BS jobs. Graeber's essay met with a wildly positive response, and people all over the world contacted him, reporting that this was exactly their situation. In light of the immense popularity of this small essay, he wrote a larger book entitled *Bullshit Jobs: A Theory*.[6]

It is important to notice that this was not a theory of bullshit, but of bullshit jobs. Yes, when one has such a job they may have to BS. However, in this book BS itself is not theorized; instead, his focus is a certain type of job. This is why Arendt's theory of bullshit, described in the last chapter, helps fill out what exactly is meant by BS. Let's look now at what Graeber means by BS jobs, and then we can discuss BS-ing at a job.

Graeber defines "a bullshit job" as

> a form of paid employment that is so completely pointless, unnecessary, or pernicious that even the employee cannot justify its existence even though, as part of the conditions of employment, the employee feels obliged to pretend that this is not the case.[7]

Graeber further offers descriptions of five types of bullshit jobs: flunkies, goons, duct tapers, box tickers, and taskmasters. Flunkies exist to help their bosses or others feel superior. Graeber says they are "unnecessary subordinates." If others weren't so insecure, this wouldn't be needed. Goons, like lawyers or lobbyists, go around threatening others and defending their boss. Duct tapers fix problems that could be fixed permanently but instead get endless temporary fixes. Box tickers do tasks that make it look like a company is doing something when it isn't really (collecting information that is then ignored, for example). Taskmasters create more work for others. Graeber calls them "unnecessary superiors."

The root of the problem with BS jobs is that in a meritocratic system we treat work as a moral task and an indicator of our moral goodness, and

---

5. David Graeber, "On the Phenomenon of Bullshit Jobs: A Work Rant."
6. David Graeber, *Bullshit Jobs: A Theory*.
7. Graeber, 9.

yet "most people hate their jobs"[8]—that is, many recognize that much of what they do is pointless or miserable and that they are completely replaceable. This is why so many start their work week already desperately waiting for Friday ("TGIF") and the tagline of one of the radio stations where I live is "helping you get through the nine to five." Graeber says he repeatedly finds in conversations with salaried professionals that they don't want to talk about their work because it is so boring. They hate their jobs, find little to no meaning in them, and develop resentment of those who do have meaningful jobs. Graeber is worth quoting at length here:

> This is a profound psychological violence here. How can one even begin to speak of dignity in labour when one secretly feels one's job should not exist? How can it not create a sense of deep rage and resentment? Yet it is the peculiar genius of our society that its rulers have figured out a way, as in the case of the fish-fryers, to ensure that rage is directed precisely against those who actually do get to do meaningful work. For instance: in our society, there seems a general rule that, the more obviously one's work benefits other people, the less one is likely to be paid for it. Again, an objective measure is hard to find, but one easy way to get a sense is to ask: what would happen were this entire class of people to simply disappear? Say what you like about nurses, garbage collectors, or mechanics, it's obvious that were they to vanish in a puff of smoke, the results would be immediate and catastrophic. A world without teachers or dock-workers would soon be in trouble, and even one without science fiction writers or ska musicians would clearly be a lesser place. It's not entirely clear how humanity would suffer were all private equity CEOs, lobbyists, PR researchers, actuaries, telemarketers, bailiffs or legal consultants to similarly vanish. (Many suspect it might markedly improve.) Yet apart from a handful of well-touted exceptions (doctors), the rule holds surprisingly well.
>
> Even more perverse, there seems to be a broad sense that this is the way things should be. This is one of the secret strengths of right-wing populism. You can see it when tabloids whip up resentment against tube workers for paralysing London during contract disputes: the very fact that tube workers can paralyse London shows that their work is actually necessary, but this seems to be precisely what annoys people. It's even clearer in the US, where Republicans have had remarkable success mobilizing resentment against school teachers, or auto workers (and not, significantly, against the school administrators or auto industry managers who actually cause the problems) for their supposedly bloated wages and benefits. It's as if they are being told "but you get to teach children! Or make cars! You get to have real jobs! And on top of that you have the nerve to also expect middle-class pensions and health care?"

8. Graeber, 241.

> If someone had designed a work regime perfectly suited to maintaining the power of finance capital, it's hard to see how they could have done a better job. Real, productive workers are relentlessly squeezed and exploited. The remainder are divided between a terrorised stratum of the, universally reviled, unemployed and a larger stratum who are basically paid to do nothing, in positions designed to make them identify with the perspectives and sensibilities of the ruling class (managers, administrators, etc.)—and particularly its financial avatars—but, at the same time, foster a simmering resentment against anyone whose work has clear and undeniable social value.[9]

BS work is suffering and stupidity but somehow deemed moral. It is as if suffering is associated with moral goodness. However, this perspective breeds resentment against those who don't have bullshit jobs. If they are happy at their work, isn't that its own reward? But, I would like to suggest, there is also sometimes a resentment here that they chose a career where they don't have to do alienating, meaningless BS. It is as if we widely associate work with BS-ing and then get angry when some choose options that don't involve BS-ing. This point requires us to synthesize Graeber's analysis with Arendt's.

BS-ing in Education, BS-ing at Work

No topic gets my university students more riled up than bullshit. I'll have students who are quiet most of the semester and then suddenly have all sorts of things to say when we start analyzing BS. The short of it is that they feel like most of their education has and continues to involve BS-ing, the jobs they have had involve BS-ing, and their careers will involve BS-ing. They hate BS-ing, they hate when others BS, they know it is morally bad for them and for society, and yet they feel trapped as if there is no way out.

In an educational setting, the students feel constantly confronted with BS and often respond by BS-ing themselves. This includes: getting assigned meaningless busywork; having to study topics they don't care about and don't see value in; having to jump through inflexible hoops, being assigned readings they don't want to do, figuring out how to either not do the reading or get the main idea without reading; getting tested on material they don't care about or dealing with exam questions that are nitpicky, irrelevant, or incoherent; figuring out how to answer questions they don't know; figuring out how to look like they know something when they don't (say, in an essay response); using ChatGPT or AI instead of writing themselves; impressing a teacher by pretending they care; shaping themselves to standards that are one-size-fits-all; and so forth.

9. Graeber, "On the Phenomenon of Bullshit Jobs: A Work Rant."

The more money is involved, the greater measures of success will be put in place, the greater the pressures to succeed will be, and the greater the temptation and necessity to BS. In general, as one reaches high school these pressures increase. Performance starts to matter because it will affect college admissions. If a child has been allowed to be a kid (let live and play without heavy control and expectation of efforts to get ahead), this becomes more difficult in high school. GPA will matter. Sports matter. Extracurriculars matter. The social scientist Douglas Campbell has pointed out that as all these issues start to matter more and are measured more, the resulting quantified standards will then form a performance loop in which the standards are known by the students and their parents, who will then proceed to try and game them. Thus, what he calls Campbell's Law:

> The more any quantitative social indicator is used for social decision-making, the more subject it will be to corruption pressures and the more apt it will be to distort and corrupt the social processes it is intended to monitor.[10]

When the students know the hoops, they will try to figure out how to look the best while exerting the minimum amount of effort possible. Some years ago, I participated in a program that had university professors teaching university courses at a local high school to give the students a chance to "get ahead," see what a college course is like, and get college credit. The course I taught was during "A hour," before the regular school schedule started. It thus attracted some of the students who were the most aggressive about their education and careers. Sadly, this meant that many were far more interested in their grades than in the material. When I handed out the take-home essay exam for the first midterm, four or five students immediately dropped the course. They took one look at the amount of work the midterm would take and decided it wasn't worth their time. One told me he had realized he was going to study something different than he had previously thought and that the course I was teaching was no longer relevant. When one student cheated on the test and was caught, the high school asked me to give her another chance, arguing explicitly to me that the course didn't really matter and what mattered was getting college credit. When I refused, they allowed her to drop the course with no penalties.

According to Campbell's Law, once measures are established, many of those who want to succeed will shift their efforts to perform well on those measures. Whole cottage industries develop around scoring well on standardized tests like the SAT, ACT, GRE, and LSAT. Students begin

10. Donald T. Campbell, "Assessing the impact of planned social change."

shaping their activities and efforts around what will look good on college entrance exams. This system encourages them to find the easiest teachers, find the easiest major based on the career or post-graduate work, and get into the best programs. These strategic efforts aren't just about how to get ahead; they are focused on how to get ahead with the minimum amount of time and effort needed. Once, in graduate school I found myself walking behind two students who were attending a course in which I was an assistant. I overheard the first say to the second, "Do you want to know how to get the best grade in a humanities course?" I admit, I was curious what he would say. "On the first essay you turn in, give your absolute best effort. If you do well, this will cement a good impression in the mind of the teacher. Then, on future essays you can spend less time on them and do less good work, but the grader will be biased and will tend to give you a better grade." Sneaky student, this probably works!

My point is not that this kind of behavior is new. Efforts to butter up the teacher have probably always existed. Rather, the point is that as life becomes about money, a career becomes the key ways to make money, and education becomes critical to getting a high-paying career, then education becomes, as Campbell says, subject to corruption pressures. Many students and many workers are constantly and strategically looking for ways to get ahead, ways to BS the BS.

To return to my university students, when I discuss this with them, they all recognize this situation. Almost all admit they have BS-ed at some point. At one end of the spectrum there is frank cheating. At the other end, there is trying to look like you know what you are talking about on a test response question even though you do not. One of the things that interests the students is how much I, as a teacher, feel like I can see it when they are BS-ing. I often mention to them that I can't tell for sure whether a student who says they really like a course while the course is ongoing is telling the truth or not. They could be saying it and really mean it, or they could be saying it to make me happy and bias me toward giving them an overall better grade. I mention that if a student tells me they dislike a course while it is ongoing, I believe them, because there is nothing to gain from saying this and even potentially much to lose. Alternatively, if I run across a student after a course is over and they tell me they liked the course, I believe them, because there is no potential ulterior motive for them to say this (unless, I suppose, they are planning on taking another course from me).

Interestingly, I have experimented with this in the past by opening a course with a discussion of BS and then telling the students I want to create a space as free from BS as possible. However, when I ask them how this can be done, they tend to be stumped. They are so used to having to be strategic and calculative that they struggle to articulate what a non-strategic space in a university setting would even look like. More than this, I have found that most actively resist trying to create a BS-free zone—they want a quantified, visible space of assignments and grading. One of the things that annoys them the most is that I don't post all their grades online and in an algorithm that will calculate their estimated current grade. Many are frank with me that they want to know this so they can estimate how much effort they should give to get the grade they want.

Obviously, these sorts of strategic and calculative maneuverings are not limited to educational settings; many people approach their careers and their jobs in this same fashion. Anyone who has worked in a professional setting is aware of the delicate dance between bosses and workers, the efforts of the bosses to extract the most labor from workers while keeping them happy or at least not disgruntled. And, on the other side of things, the efforts of many workers to do the least amount of work necessary to keep their bosses happy. Or, alternatively, the efforts of workers to look like they care and are the best workers in order to get promotions, bonuses, and other perks.

The places many of us spend most of our time are not BS-free but rather BS-full spaces. This is what smells so bad to the students. It reeks. They know it, but they know no way out. Some of them just embrace it. Ironically, they almost all agree—even those who seem to enjoy the game—that BS is harmful to themselves and others. They believe that they are not being true to themselves, that they are having to warp themselves to fit alien and often absurd expectations, and that all this is morally damaging. Pop culture is filled with media decrying this situation: *Severance*, *Fight Club*, *Dilbert*, *Office Space*, *The Office*, *They Live*—on and on—restaurants named TGIF, radio stations promising to help them survive their day at work, much of our language about the workweek (Monday is miserable, Wednesday is "hump day," Friday finally, the weekend is respite). It is wildly inhuman, and yet no one seems to know what else we could do.

The Moral Fallout: Accepting Irrationality, Compromising Integrity, Thoughtlessness

Let me return to Arendt to discuss one way of understanding why this is so morally damaging.

Money is abstract and inhuman. Money systems are not about human well-being but exist for the accumulation of money. This means that from the perspective of human well-being, common sense morality, and even proportional economies, money systems are irrational.

This is clearly apparent from the perspective of premodern and non-modern peoples. Take for example a story about money related to the anthropologist James Suzman by /Engn!au of the Ju/'hoan San:

> Jackal had been riding his donkey and grew tired, so he decided to stop and cook some meat. Once his food was getting hot, he saw some farmers coming toward him and quickly put out the fire. When the farmers arrived, he said, "Look! This is a magic pot. It doesn't need a fire to cook food. You must just hit it three times." He did just that, and then showed the farmers the meat that was still sizzling. "I will sell you this magic pot for $1,000," said Jackal. They took him up on the offer.
>
> Later, the farmers grew hungry and tested their new pot. But after hitting it three times, they found their meat was still raw. They tried again—still raw. Realizing they'd been tricked, they went back to Jackal, who was scared to see his customers returning. Quickly, he took the money they had given him for the pot and hid it in his donkey's rear end.
>
> The farmers demanded their money back. "I can't," replied Jackal. "This pot is yours now. Anyway, I have already spent the money." But just as he said this, the donkey farted and all the money tumbled from its backside. For a second Jackal was terrified, but then he smiled. "Look at this donkey," he said to the farmers. "It's magic because if you feed it grass, it will shit money." He offered it to the farmers for $1,000. "This is a magic donkey!" agreed the farmers. So they parted with another thousand dollars, and Jackal happily went on his way.[11]

According to Suzman, we learn four things from this: "that money is created by magic; that it is acquired through trickery and deceit; that it inspires greed, violence, fear, possessiveness, and anger; that it often appears to come from assholes and is covered in shit."[12]

Even occasionally now we find events that we struggle to explain or justify rationally. Take, for example, the case of Haliey Welch, a young woman from Nashville, Tennessee, who quickly went viral as the "Hawk Tuah Girl" after a video of her making a vulgar sexual joke was posted online. Welch proceeded to quickly make various trademarks, including a podcast called Talk Tuah, and generate merchandise based on the viral video. Some estimates were that her net worth from the resulting fame quickly went above a million dollars. Then, oddly, Welch tried to launch

---

11. James Suzman, "When a 200,000-Year-Old Culture Encountered the Modern Economy."

12. James Suzman, *Affluence Without Abundance: What We Can Learn from the World's Most Successful Civilisation*, 243.

a meme cryptocurrency called HAWK that took off for a brief moment before crashing, resulting in some people losing their life savings after investing in it.

Everything about this is absurd and makes no more sense than Vanilla Ice making millions of dollars doing nothing in real estate. Unsurprisingly, there were many bitter complaints online that Hawk Tuah Girl made more money from a stupid comment about oral sex than they could make in a year doing honest work. But, at the same time, there are hordes of people out there recording themselves doing all sorts of silly things and posting it online in an effort to go viral and hit it big.

Another example of the disturbing disconnect between honest work and disproportional work comes from public school teachers making millions on OnlyFans, a subscription website primarily known for hosting and selling self-made pornography.[13] It cuts out the middle man (except for the website of course) and allows users to subscribe directly to creators. Since the rise of OnlyFans, there have been quite a few cases of "regular" people hitting it big and making millions of dollars. Particularly striking are public school teachers who struggle to get by doing something that is, they believe, to be very important and turn to OnlyFans as a side hustle that for some pays significantly more than what they are being paid to teach. Sometimes a local community finds out, and the teacher is fired from their job. Stories like this make news headlines because of the contrast between a public school teacher and a porn star; however, these stories tend to focus on the salacious click-bait narrative rather than the poor pay that leads to it.

Despite the absurdity of the bizarre ways to make money doing nonsense or jumping through hoops at a BS job, many embrace this madness because it works. If you want to get wealthy you have to take advantage of disproportional means to get money. These are abstract and from a commonsense perspective, irrational. In the end, one must accept an irrational game, play by the irrational rules of that game, and win. The absurdity and irrationality of it all must be ignored or transformed into something rational through some kind of ideological magic.

Often these games make sense when one knows the rules and is immersed in the game. Take American football for example. It is infamous for having bizarre rules that make little sense from an outsider perspective. It is also a particularly dangerous sport, resulting in traumatic brain

13. Emily Van de Riet, "Former Teacher Said She Has Made Nearly $1 Million from Onlyfans in Less Than 6 Months."

damage and other chronic injuries for many players. Some, most famously Junior Seau, commit suicide after leaving the league as a result of developing chronic traumatic encephalopathy from their playing days. And yet, the NFL is the most profitable sports league in the United States and is so popular that some have compared it to a religion. For those who play the game or watch it, football can be life. In some communities, Friday night high school football is the primary form of community gathering. For some fans, Saturdays are devoted to college football and Sunday to the NFL. Of course, Monday Night Football has long been a staple, and the Superbowl is the highlight of the year for many and treated as if it were a national holiday. All of this is suffused with money. College football has recently allowed players to get endorsements. Top recruits make millions at the age of eighteen. They jump schools as opportunities and money become better elsewhere. Universities make football coaches the highest paid individuals on the university payroll and increasingly "buy" the best recruits. University stadiums and sports facilities attract far more investment than the rest of the campus and programs. From the outside, all this can appear like an absolute and weirdly obscure mania. It is wildly disproportional for people to make massive amounts of money for throwing a ball.

Much of the business world is driven by these same kinds of games. Take, for example, a series of ads run by SAP, a German software company that provides business solutions. In one of these ads, a man sits at an outdoor bar on a beach overlooking the ocean. With a newspaper in hand, he turns to camera and says, "Looks like this year's big gift took everyone by surprise. Hopefully not the CFL. Now with SAP, AI could have a plan to meet demand. So it's happy holidays in the C-suit." In another ad in the same series, the same man sits near a pool at the same luxury location and, looking up from his newspaper, says: "Did you catch this on page seven? The world is still running short on AI chips. Uff, that problem is not going anywhere anytime soon. Got to feel for those COOs. But if they have SAP then they planned ahead. Probably more concerned with this little tidbit back on page twelve: 'Patchy snowfall on the slopes this weekend.' You hate to see it. A little fresh pow pow too much to ask?"

There are more similar ads in this series, all featuring the same wealthy-looking gentleman at an oceanside resort, relaxing and speaking to the viewer through the camera in inscrutable business speak.

What the man is saying is intended to be obscure and inaccessible to a normal person. He lives and works in a world that normal people can't understand. The reward for entering this world is wealth: the man casually speaks of the quality of the snow powder. In another ad, he speaks of throwing an end-of-year party at his office.

These ads have the performative effects of excluding or including the viewer depending on how initiated they are into this business world. To the uninitiated, it is not going to be clear what he is talking about. He speaks in business lingo. And yet, it will be clear to the outsider that he is wealthy.

As an outsider, these ads are incredibly annoying. They are essentially mocking the uninitiated. They throw you into the business world and hint at the great wealth that exists for those who play these games, and they do so by pushing the inscrutable language right in your face. Don't speak this? That's why you are not rich, like us.

The odd thing is, there is also a palpable sense of how absurd this is. As Karen Ho points out in her ethnography of Wall Street, the actual daily tasks for most those who work in the business world are boring "shit work" and "number crunching."[14] Contrary to their "culture of smartness," in which they portray themselves as smarter than the rest of the fools who don't know how to play the game of business, Ho finds Wall Street to be full of intense conformity, schmoozing, and bullshitting.[15] The business lingo of the gentleman in the SAP ads reflects this inanity. He is rich because he is smart, speaks the lingo, and knows how to play the game. But, it is also apparent from his exasperation with the inane tasks he has to manage that this is a silly game.

Arendt's claim is that BS-ing, especially compromising one's integrity to submit to irrational games or systems, has terrible moral consequences for those who do so, and, when they are in positions of influence or power, for the rest of us too. Oddly, this soul-destroying damage is tacitly recognized when it comes to work. As Graeber points out, often jobs are associated with suffering, absurdity, alienation and irrationality—and yet putting up with this is taken as a sign of virtue.[16] Putting up with BS or BS-ing oneself is mistaken as a substitute for or a part of hard work. If a job involves BS, and a job is work, then BS-ing is a form of work. If work is a sign of one's discipline and virtue, then so is putting up with BS.

But as we saw for Hannah Arendt, constantly submitting yourself to irrational imperatives or performing for superiors threatens to hollow you out. It can leave a shell of an individual who is so accustomed to doing

14. Karen Ho, *Liquidated: An Ethnography of Wall Street*, 99.

15. Ho, 52, 73.

16. Graeber, *Bullshit Jobs: A Theory*.

what they are told and smiling for the cameras that they become thoughtless. Recall that by "thoughtlessness" Arendt doesn't mean not using one's brain. Like Eichmann, we can be very good at performing tasks that require cognition (problem-solving) while failing to think through the morality of what we are doing. Indeed, when Arendt claims thoughtlessness is one of the defining characteristics of our time, she is worrying that we are educating and training ourselves into little Adolf Eichmanns.

Another way of putting this point would be to say that we become good at accepting and working within a given framework (cognition), but bad at questioning the framework itself (thinking as wonder). The result is a thoughtless competence. The problem, of course, becomes what happens when we put thoughtless but competent individuals into inhuman systems or games, like, as Arendt would point to, Nazi Germany. We are inclined to think competence is a good thing, but when it is combined with thoughtlessness or the inability to critically question the morality of the system or frame it is in, it can result in the highly effective machinery of the Holocaust.

Much of the intense criticism aimed at Arendt from *Eichmann in Jerusalem* is that she implied that this kind of thoughtless competence was not just present in Nazi Germany; it is in much of the modern world. The last thing readers wanted to find is that they were being compared to Eichmann, but Arendt saw thoughtlessness all around her.

One mark of and also a result of this thoughtlessness is what La Boétie famously called "voluntary servitude."[17] This can take many forms, but here I am thinking of the way that one must submit to an exploitative game or system to gain access to wealth in a disproportional economy. Of course, it is often not enough merely to play the game; you must also excel. Frédéric Gros has coined the term "surplus obedience" to describe the ways in which we can go above and beyond the minimum acceptable levels of obedience.[18] This could be servile obsequiousness to bosses, but it may also be striving to be the best at completing the BS tasks that make up much of disproportional work. Thus, we find ourselves working the longest hours, being the most aggressive, and hitting the highest numbers—all to climb up that ladder.

To be so committed to BS involves high levels of cognition but willful ignorance of how unnatural and unintuitive these systems can be. Among

---

17. See the discussion of La Boétie in Frédéric Gros, *Disobey!: A Philosophy of Resistance.*

18. Gros.

the results of this thoughtlessness is the painful inability to see the absurdity of the world of bullshit that we have created. Our lives are riddled with contradictions that we can't seem to see. The foundation of the American economy is immigrant labor, and yet immigrants are the target of seemingly endless vitriol. Many public school teachers can't get paid enough to get by, unless they turn to OnlyFans or other secondary BS jobs, while speculators make millions from memecoins.

I can't help but think of the alarmed criticism of Osage Chief Big Soldier in 1820:

> I see and admire your manner of living, your good warm houses; your extensive fields of corn, your gardens, your cows, oxen, workhouses, wagons, and a thousand machines that I know not the use of. I see that you are able to clothe yourselves, even from weeds and grass. In short, you even do almost what you choose. You whites possess the power of subduing almost every animal to your use. You are surrounded by slaves. Everything about you is in chains, and you are slaves yourselves. I fear if I should exchange my pursuits for yours, I too should become a slave.[19]

Big Soldier recognizes that the Western way of living does indeed produce many impressive consumer goods, but he concludes that the price to pay is far too high. It involves reducing the world to servitude. And Big Soldier is not alone in this reaction. David Graeber and David Wengrow point out that not only were many Indigenous Americans horrified at Western practices, many Westerners who were captured or raised in Indigenous American communities preferred them to Western ones:

> Some emphasized the virtues of freedom they found in Native American societies, including sexual freedom, but also freedom from the expectation of constant toil in pursuit of land or wealth. Others noted the "Indian's" reluctance ever to let anyone fall into a condition of poverty, hunger or destitution. . . . [T]hey found life infinitely more pleasant in a society where no one else was in a position of abject misery. . . .
>
> Still others noted the ease with which outsiders, taken in by "Indian" families, might achieve acceptance and prominent positions in their adoptive communities, becoming members of chiefly households, or even chiefs themselves. Western propagandists speak endlessly about equality of opportunity [meritocracy]; these seem to have been societies where it actually existed. By far the most common reasons, however, had to do with the intensity of social bonds they experienced in Native American communities; qualities of mutual care, love and above all happiness, which they found impossible to replicate once back in European settings. . . .

19. Vine Deloria Jr., *Spirit and Reason: The Vine Deloria, Jr., Reader*, 4.

> One gets the sense that indigenous life was, to put it very crudely, just a lot more interesting than life in a "Western" town or city, especially insofar as the latter involved long hours of monotonous, repetitive, conceptually empty activity. The fact that we find it hard to imagine how such an alternative life could be endlessly engaging and interesting is perhaps more a reflection on the limits of our imagination than on the life itself.[20]

To summarize these claims: Western consumerism is deeply unfree, unbearably aporophobic, unmeritocratic, alienating, stupefying, and boring. As I've stressed before, some of these criticisms are widely recognized in the West itself—the alienating, stultifying suffering of many jobs is taken precisely as a sign that they are hard work and that submitting to them is virtuous. However, the Indigenous critique correctly calls BS. None of this is ennobling. It is spiritually damaging to everyone involved. Critically, the Indigenous critique cuts right to the heart of Western pretensions—not only is it a moral disaster, it also isn't meritocratic at all. It is caught up in disproportionate nonsense.

In short, Western consumerism is bad. It fails not only from the perspective of grace or a proportional economy, but also in terms of its own meritocratic ideals. We do not live in a meritocracy; instead, we are in a bizarre disproportional economy where many are trying to shortcut their way to wealth—in fact, there is no other way to wealth. You can't honest your way to riches. Worse, Western consumerism produces a kind of thoughtlessness that results in an inability to imagine alternatives. This is particularly striking in the case of the Latter-day Saint tradition, which scripturally has powerful and dramatic counter-capitalist ideals of an order of grace, which will be articulated and advocated for in the conclusion.

---

20. David Graeber and David Wengrow, *The Dawn of Everything: A New History of Humanity*, 20–21.

Conclusions

Abraham's near-sacrifice of Isaac is often held up as the quintessential trial of faith. In fact, I was told many times as a youth that each and every one of us would have to go through some sort of Abrahamic test so that God could know if each of us would be obedient to Him.

There are, it seems to me, different kinds of trials of faith. When Nephi is asked to kill Laban in the opening chapters of the Book of Mormon, his response is quite different from Abraham's. Rather than immediately complying, Nephi shrinks back. He doesn't understand why God would command him to do something—to kill someone—when God had explicitly made the sixth of the Ten Commandments "Thou shalt not kill" (Ex. 20:13). When he questions this, "the Spirit" provides him with a logical explanation, and subsequently Nephi does the deed (1 Ne. 4:7–18).

The sacrifice of Isaac occurs on the register of obedience. Will Abraham do whatever God asks, even if it seems to contradict what God has said and done previously (fulfill a promise about Abraham's posterity)? Abraham was going to do it, but Nephi hesitates and questions before being given a clear explanation. Why isn't Nephi's trial of faith one that we focus on? Alarmingly, in my opinion, not only do we not focus on this trial of faith in which questioning seems to be the right response, we have turned Nephi into another figure of strict obedience. (As Latter-day Saint children sing in Primary, "I will go, I will do, the things the Lord commands"—while omitting this important part of the narrative.) Perhaps one trial is whether we will obey (I actually think obedience is a poor way to relate to God), but another is what we will do when confronted with an immoral command.

There is, however, another trial of faith directly posed by Jesus in the Sermon on the Mount:

> Therefore I say unto you, Take no thought for your life, what ye shall eat, or what ye shall drink; nor yet for your body, what ye shall put on. Is not the life more than meat, and the body than raiment?
>
> Behold the fowls of the air: for they sow not, neither do they reap, nor gather into barns; yet your heavenly Father feedeth them. Are ye not much better than they?
>
> Which of you by taking thought can add one cubit unto his stature?
>
> And why take ye thought for raiment? Consider the lilies of the field, how they grow; they toil not, neither do they spin:
>
> And yet I say unto you, That even Solomon in all his glory was not arrayed like one of these.

> Wherefore, if God so clothe the grass of the field, which today is, and tomorrow is cast into the oven, shall he not much more clothe you, O ye of little faith? (Matt. 6:25–30)

In Chapter 2, I called this an "invitation" to the order of grace, but that is probably too light of a way to put it. Jesus instead presents this as a challenge ("O ye of little faith?") and frames it as a commandment. Rather than merely suggesting this, he makes it an imperative: "Take no thought for your life, what ye shall eat, or what ye shall drink; nor yet for your body, what ye shall put on."

I remember reading this when I was younger and dwelling on how difficult it was. "Take no thought." Stop calculating. Stop planning. Stop worrying. Life is a gift, and it should be lived as something gifted rather than turning it into a matter of work and earning. Embrace abundance. Live gracefully.

This is hard for us in modern life when we are so highly propagandized into scarcity and so moralized into merit with messages instructing that we must earn our way and pay our part. That is how we prove we merit salvation—after all we can do.

And yet, if we take heavenly abundance seriously and look at our own irrational, disproportionate, aporophobic world of bullshit through the lens of grace, the command to be like the lilies should be deeply attractive.

In a secular context, arguing for the historical existence of existential abundance and the logic of grace is often met with resistance. This doesn't fit with our modern (propagandistic) narratives of prehistory. However, in the Latter-day Saint context grace is not only laced throughout scripture, but there are powerful examples of living the order of grace. I am thinking in particular of the two centuries and peace and egalitarianism told in 4 Nephi. Here we find a community that established abundance and grace here on Earth:

> And they had all things common among them; therefore there were not rich and poor, bond and free, but they were all made free, and partakers of the heavenly gift. (4 Ne. 1:3)

For roughly two hundred years they were able to maintain this:

> And it came to pass that there was no contention in the land, because of the love of God which did dwell in the hearts of the people. And there were no envyings, nor strifes, nor tumults, nor whoredoms, nor lyings, nor murders, nor any manner of lasciviousness; and surely there could not be a happier people among all the people who had been created by the hand of God. (vv. 15–16)

Like most of us raised in modernity, I have been shaped to think in utilitarian terms. And utilitarianism is explicitly about maximizing happiness (or the greatest amount of good or pleasure). When I first read in the Book of Mormon about the happiest people that had existed in the history of humankind, it seemed clear to me this is what we should be striving for. After all, as Latter-day Saints like to emphasize, "Men are, that they might have joy" (2 Ne. 2:25). If we are meant to have joy, why not maximize that joy like good utilitarians? However, this is a communal task that cannot be done alone or with leaving others behind. If the widow and the orphan are not taken care of, then grace is compromised.

This account in the Book of Mormon doesn't just describe the happiest community in the existence of humankind but also how it ended:

> And now, in this two hundred and first year there began to be among them those who were lifted up in pride, such as the wearing of costly apparel, and all manner of fine pearls, and of the fine things of the world.
>
> And from that time forth they did have their goods and their substance no more common among them.
>
> And they began to be divided into classes; and they began to build up churches unto themselves to get gain, and began to deny the true church of Christ. (4 Ne. 1:24–26)

Predictably, the enemy of the happiest community is money and the rejection of grace for individual honors.

It seems to me that 4 Nephi should play a much larger role in the Latter-day Saint cultural imagination than it does. Its relative absence is telling and reflects the hegemony of meritocracy. Unfortunately, and this is the overarching claim of this book, grace and money are incommensurable. The logic of money works against the logic of grace. The scarcity of meritocracy undermines the abundance of heaven. God or Mammon—you can't have both.

We must choose either grace or money. But what does this actually look like at a practical level? Are we actually supposed to not use money? Is that even possible?

Money is not just a neutral tool, but rather, as I've argued, a social logic or a social order. The order of money radically shapes our moral imagination. A first step to turning away from money toward grace would therefore be to understand how the order of money affects our identity, behavior, and thinking. Second, and related to the first step, is to articulate an alternative. As the saying goes, the fish doesn't know it is in water, and so we have to get out of the "money" water. If I am correct that the order of grace is the opposite of the order of money, then grace is a critically important source of "seeing" differently. This book is an attempt to initiate this critique.

While I have offered suggestions and examples of living (more) gracefully at various points throughout this book, I want to finish by discussing both the practicality and impracticality of trying to live more gracefully. A practical approach to grace will be incrementalist and, because it takes small steps, it risks being reinscribed in the logic of money. But, of course, small steps are less daunting. Emphasizing the radically different nature of the order of grace, on the other hand, and therefore the impracticality of living gracefully, runs the risk of overwhelming us right off the bat; however, it might be precisely the kind of thing that will get us to take a leap of faith instead of pussyfooting.

By beginning with practical, small steps approaches to grace, I am trying to speak to two groups. The first are those who are genuinely interested in trying to live a more graceful life but who might appreciate concrete examples of what that might look like. The second are skeptics who will doubt any idealistic suggestions unless they are given concrete, practical examples. Sometimes this kind of skepticism is disingenuous and made in bad faith (for example, when gun advocates expect their interlocutors to know specific details about different kinds of guns that don't really matter, but which are then used as a silly excuse to claim interlocutors don't know what they are talking about), but concrete examples can be helpful for genuinely open skeptics.

With that said, as I began writing these practical suggestions down, a fascinating tension became quickly apparent. Some of these suggestions seem to be commonsensical—like the claim we should be grateful. But almost always when a way of living gracefully appears as common sense or already familiar, this tends to mean we have assimilated it into the order of money in a watered-down version. When we try to move away from the order of money toward the order of grace, imperatives like gratitude change their tone. So, the quotidian "be grateful" now comes along with the imperative to share and not keep what we have been given for ourselves. Gratitude that sits on the gift now becomes innocuous and hollow.

Thus, what follows should be thought of as an indication that we can move in the direction of grace, but that in doing so we will increasingly see how radically different the order of grace is from the order of money's status quo:

- We should recognize that everything we have is a gift from God, that we don't earn it, and that it is not ours.
- We should feel gratitude for what we have been given.
- Because the ethics of giving requires we not stop the flow of gifts, those we receive should turn our gaze toward others. We should look for the widow and the orphan, for those in need, and help lift them up.
- Inversely, we should not tolerate inequality. Those who hoard the abundance for themselves endanger not only themselves but also the rest of us.
- As such, we should stop idealizing wannabe alphas that pillage and plunder the poor for their own gain. They are the villains, not the heroes.
- To live in a large house or wear nice clothing while others go hungry is evil.
- We should recognize our aporophobic, segregated neighborhoods as cruel and destructive.
- While the order of money in modern life is generally individualistic, it is often comparative in that it signals that one can attain what others cannot. (For example, name-brand clothing or luxury items are often purchased to "stand out.") Conversely, the order of grace is social and comparative in that it looks out for those who have less in order to lift them up and bring them closer.
- Thus, while the order of money can insist that you "mind your own business," the order of grace cannot. On the contrary, grace must pay attention to the conditions of all those around us.
- This means that there are different kinds of freedom at work in each. In terms of the differences between them, in the order of money we have the freedom to do what we want with what is "ours" (the freedom to exclude others) and the freedom to be left alone, while in the order of grace we have the freedom from alphas and the injustices and slaveries that come with the world of money to the detriment of others.
- We need to reject the divinization of work. Work is not necessarily good. Work that is alienating, stultifying, and demeaning is often spiritually damaging. We should seek to minimize psychological and spiritual harm.
- We need to put humans and human well-being before abstract systems. Money especially has a tendency to breed itself, and systems driven by money tend to end up just being centered on money.
- Disproportional economics can create odd benefits but are dangerous unless an entire community can profit from them.

- These bizarre proliferations of money are often irrational from a traditional perspective. We need to avoid accommodating ourselves to irrationalities and BS. Abstract inhuman systems warp human thinking and human behavior. They can result in thoughtlessness.
- It can also result in a predatory, entrepreneurial approach to life and to the world around us. Instead of seeing the world as a gift, the world is seen as a source of potential resources that can be used to make money. This is an exploitative mentality, and it is destroying the earth.
- As such, living according to the order of grace requires rethinking our relationship with the earth.
- While I emphasized the failure of our modern world in human terms in the last chapter, we can also frame it in nonhuman terms. Consider, for example, the following scriptures from the book of Moses:

> And it came to pass that Enoch looked upon the earth; and he heard a voice from the bowels thereof, saying: Wo, wo is me, the mother of men; I am pained, I am weary, because of the wickedness of my children. When shall I rest, and be cleansed from the filthiness which is gone forth out of me? When will my Creator sanctify me, that I may rest, and righteousness for a season abide upon my face?
>
> And when Enoch heard the earth mourn, he wept, and cried unto the Lord, saying: O Lord, wilt thou not have compassion upon the earth? (Moses 7:48–49)

- The gratitude and love we should feel in the order of grace should extend to the nonhuman world. Be kind to animals. Protect the environment. Care for the earth. Culturally, Latter-day Saints have been embarrassingly terrible in this regard.
- This kind of relationship is closer to how feminist care ethics has described caring or maternal thinking.[1] It is not one based on competition and agonism; instead it seeks peace and mutual fruition.
- If that sounds saccharine, keep in mind that the relative equality of hunter-gatherers was achieved by dominating the would-be dominators—killing the alphas if necessary.
- We also need to be attentive to and seek to undo the influence of alpha-male "warrior" thinking, including the image of the Christian warrior-God—what Georg Baudler calls the "Christian God of terror."[2]

---

1. Sara Ruddick, *Maternal Thinking: Towards a Politics of Peace.*

2. Georg Baudler, *God and Violence: The Christian Experience of God in Dialogue with Myths and Other Religions*, 109.

These are just some initial suggestions. Some are more radical and potentially impractical; others can be quite accessible. Be kind to plants and animals, avoid luxury goods, condemn the love of money, talk about inequality, defend immigrants, resist meritocratic narratives and justifications, suffer with the poor, feel ashamed of inequality. Read from Indigenous authors that live in more graceful cultures than our own.

Having offered some concrete examples of small steps we can take toward grace, let me make one final emphasis on how radically different it is from the order of money. In his 2014 book, *Debt: The First 5,000 Years*, David Graeber offers an important but brief discussion of calculability and redemption. He writes,

> The refusal to calculate credits and debts can be found throughout the anthropological literature on egalitarian hunting societies. Rather than seeing himself as human because he could make economic calculations, the hunter insisted that being truly human meant *refusing* to make such calculations, refusing to measure or remember who had given what to whom, for the precise reason that doing so would inevitably create a world where we begin "comparing power with power, measuring, calculating" and reducing each other to slaves or dogs through debt.[3]

Quantification, calculation, and accounting either belong to or will tend toward the order of money. They invite competition and agonism. They invite predatory lending and usury. Graeber points out that redemption or salvation in the Bible is about freeing someone who is in debt. We have to keep in mind that the Bible repeatedly illustrates that

> this is what money meant to the majority of people for most of human history: the terrifying prospect of one's sons and daughters being carried off to the homes of repulsive strangers to clean their pots and provide occasional sexual services, to be subject to every conceivable form of violence and abuse, possibility for years, conceivably forever.[4]

Redemption then, on his account, is not, as we often describe it in the order of money, merely about individual salvation; it is rather "more a matter of destroying the entire system of accounting."[5] This is a remarkable and dramatic understanding of the order of grace—one that is hard for us to comprehend. We use the word "accountability" as a synonym for responsibility. A responsible person is able to give an account of what they did, where, when, how, and why. They have control over what they have

3. David Graeber, *Debt: The First 5,000 Years*, 79.
4. Graeber, 85.
5. Graeber, 82.

done. The have calculated out the best way to get to the best results, and they have followed through. Except, as Søren Kierkegaard loves to point out, there is no risk in calculation. Or, as Friedrich Nietzsche put it:

> What? Do we really want to permit existence to be degraded for us like this—reduced to a mere exercise for a calculator and an indoor diversion for mathematicians? Above all, one should not wish to divest existence of its *rich ambiguity* . . . an interpretation that permits counting, calculation, weighing, seeing, and touching and nothing more—that is a crudity and a naiveté, assuming that it is not a mental illness, an idiocy. . . . A "scientific" interpretation of the world, as you understand it, might therefore still be one of the *most stupid* of all possible interpretations of the world, meaning that it is one of the poorest in meaning. . . . [A]n essentially mechanical world would be an essentially *meaningless* world. Assuming that one estimated the *value* of a piece of music according to how much it could be counted, calculated and expressed in formulas: how absurd would such a "scientific" estimation of music be! What would one have comprehended, understood, grasped of it? Nothing, really nothing of what is "music" in it![6]

The order of grace is full of love, full of abundance, overflowing, and incalculable. I'm not sure we can baby-step our way into it. I suspect it is so radically different that it requires a leap of faith. A leap out of the order of money, into the order of grace. This is not to say baby steps can't move us in that direction; it is just that small steps are almost always small because they are calculated.

No wonder when many Indigenous people look at our modern world, they see it as a critically and morally impoverished one. We live in an irrational, disproportionate, aporophobic world of bullshit that we should find intolerable. When the president of the United States promises mass deportations, Christians should have been the loudest and most aggressive defenders of migrants. Unfortunately, Latter-day Saints were not. This is just one of many indications of the ways that a murderous order of money has captured and damaged our moral imagination and the quality of our lives. We have embraced an ugly meritocracy that makes a mockery of grace. I hope this book contributes to making us ashamed of these failures and turning us toward a more grace-full existence.

6. Friedrich Nietzsche, *The Gay Science*, aphorism 373.

Bibliography

Abram, David. *The Spell of the Sensuous*. Vintage Books, 1997.

Agnew, Jean-Christophe. *World Apart: The Market and the Theater in Ango-American Thought, 1550–1750*. Cambridge University Press, 1993.

Anzaldúa, Gloria. *Borderlands/La Frontera: The New Mestiza*. Aunt Lute Books, 2012.

Arendt, Hannah. *Between Past and Future*. The Viking Press, 1961.

———. *Eichmann in Jerusalem*. Penguin Classics, 2006.

———. *The Human Condition*. University of Chicago Press, 1998.

———. *The Life of the Mind*. Harcourt Brace and Company, 1978.

———. *On Revolution*. Penguin Classics, 2006.

———. *The Origins of Totalitarianism*. Schocken Books, 1951.

Aristotle. *Politics*. Translated by H. Rackham. Harvard University Press, 1932.

Baudler, Georg. *God and Violence: The Christian Experience of God in Dialogue with Myths and Other Religions*. Templegate Publishers, 1992.

Bellah, Robert N. *Religion in Human Evolution: From the Paleolithic to the Axial Age*. The Belknap Press of Harvard University Press, 2011.

Boehm, Christopher. *Hierarchy in the Forest: The Evolution of Egalitarian Behavior*. Harvard University Press, 1999.

Boldeman, Lee. *The Cult of the Market: Economic Fundamentalism and its Discontents*. ANU Press, 2011.

Bookchin, Murray. *The Ecology of Freedom:. The Emergence and Dissolution of Hierarchy*. AK Press, 2005.

Campbell, Donald T. "Assessing the impact of planned social change." *Evaluation and Program Planning* 2, no. 1 (1979): 67–90.

Clark, Christopher. *The Roots of Rural Capitalism: Western Massachusetts 1780–1860*. Cornell University Press, 1992.

Connel, R. W. *Masculinities*. University of California Press, 2005.

Cortina, Adela. *Aporophobia: Why We Reject the Poor Instead of Helping Them*. Princeton University Press, 2022.

Cox, Harvey. *The Market as God*. Harvard University Press, 2016.

Deloria Jr., Vine. *Spirit and Reason: The Vine Deloria, Jr., Reader*. Fulcrum, 1999.

Deloria Jr., Vine and Daniel Wildcat. *Power and Place: Indian Education in America*. Fulcrum, 2001.

Diaz, Daniella. "Trump: 'I'm Smart' For Not Paying Taxes."CNN.com. Updated September 27, 2016. https://www.cnn.com/2016/09/26/politics/donald-trump-federal-income-taxes-smart-debate.

Duke University. "Vanessa Woods on the 'Bonobo Handshake' {Duke University Office Hours}." YouTube. May 18, 2010. Accessed November 23, 2024. https://www.youtube.com/watch?v=5CGMJiGe6u4.

Eich, Stefan. *The Currency of Politics: The Political Theory of Money from Aristotle to Keynes*. Princeton University Press, 2023.

Flake, Kathleen. *The Politics of American Religious Identity: The Seating of Senator Reed Smoot, Mormon Apostle*. The University of North Carolina Press, 2004.

Flannery, Kant and Joyce Marcus. *The Creation of Inequality: How Our Prehistoric Ancestors Set the Stage for Monarchy, Slavery and Empire*. Harvard University Press, 2012.

FOX 13 news staff. "What Does 'Woke' Mean? Gov. Desantis Officials Answer During Andrew Warren Trial." FOX 13 News. December 5, 2022. Accessed December 12, 2023. https://www.fox13news.com/news/what-does-woke-mean-gov-desantis-officials-answer-during-andrew-warren-trial.

Frankfurt, Harry G. "Donald Trump Is BS, Says Expert in BS." TIME Magazine. May 12, 2016. Accessed July 29, 2020. https://time.com/4321036/donald-trump-bs/.

Frankfurt, Harry G. *On Bullshit*. Princeton University Press, 2005.

Fraser, Nancy and Linda Gordon. "A Genealogy of Dependency: Tracing a Keyword of the U.S. Welfare State." *Signs* 19, no. 2 (Winter 1994): 309–36.

Gadamer, Hans-Georg. *Truth and Method*. Continuum, 1996.

Godbout, Jacques T. and Alain Caillé. *The World of the Gift*. McGill-Queen's University Press, 1998.

Graeber, David. *Bullshit Jobs: A Theory*. Simon and Schuster, 2019.

———. "Culture as Creative Refusal." *The Cambridge Journal of Anthropology* 31, no. 2 (Autumn 2013): 1–19.

———. *Debt: The First 5,000 Years*. Melville House, 2014.

———. "On the Phenomenon of Bullshit Jobs: A Work Rant." STRIKE! Magazine. August 2013. Accessed January 1, 2025. https://strikemag.org/bullshit-jobs/.

———. *The Utopia of Rules*. Melville House, 2015.

Graeber, David and David Wengrow. *The Dawn of Everything: A New History of Humanity*. Farrar, Straus and Giroux, 2021.

Griffin, Lauren. "Trump Isn't Lying, He's Bullshitting—And It's Far More Dangerous." The Conversation. January 26, 2017. Accessed July 29, 2020. https://theconversation.com/trump-isnt-lying-hes-bullshitting-and-its-far-more-dangerous-71932.

Gros, Frédéric. *Disobey!: A Philosophy of Resistance*. Verso, 2021.

Hénaff, Marcel. *The Price of Truth: Gift, Money and Philosophy*. Stanford University Press, 2010.

Heshel, Abraham. *The Prophets*. Perennial Classics, 2001.

Ho, Karen. *Liquidated: An Ethnography of Wall Street*. Duke University Press, 2009.

Hochschild, Arlie Russell. *The Commercialization of Intimate Life: Notes from Home and Work*. University of California Press, 2003.

———. *The Managed Heart: Commercialization of Human Feeling*. University of California Press, 2003.

Hudson, Michael *...And Forgive Them Their Debts: Lending, Foreclosure and Redemption from Bronze Age Finance to the Jubilee Year*. ISLET Verlag-Dresdan, 2018.

Hyde, Lewis. *The Gift: Imagination and the Erotic Life of Property*. Vintage Books, 1983.

Illing, Sean. "A 1951 Book About Totalitarianism Is Flying Off the Shelves. Here's Why." Vox. Updated January 30, 2019. Accessed July 29, 2020. www.vox.com/conversations/2017/6/28/15829712/hannah-arendt-donald-trump-brexit-totalitarianism.

Jonas, Hans. *The Imperative of Responsibility: In Search of an Ethics of a Technological Age*. University of Chicago Press, 1985.

Kaye, Joel. *Economy and Nature in the Fourteenth Century: Money, Market Exchange and the Emergence of Scientific Thought*. Cambridge University Press, 1998.

Kimmerer, Robin Wall. *Braiding Sweetgrass: Indigenous Wisdom, Scientific Knowledge and the Teaching of Plants*. Milkweed Editions, 2015.

———. *Gathering Moss: A Natural and Cultural History of Mosses*. Oregon State University Press, 2003.

Le Goff, Jacques. *Money and the Middle Ages: An Essay in Historical Anthropology*. Polity Press, 2012.

Mauss, Marcel. *The Gift: The Form and Reason for Exchange in Archaic Societies*. W. W. Norton Company, 2000.

McCarraher, Eugene. *The Enchantments of Mammon: How Capitalism became the Religion of Modernity*. Belknap Press, 2019.

McNally, David. *Blood and Money: War Slavery, Finance, and Empire*. Haymarket Books, 2020.

Moruzzi, Norma. "From Parvenu to Pariah: Hannah Arendt's *Rahel Varnhagen*." In *Heidegger's Jewish Followers*, edited by Samuel Fleischacker. Duquesne Press, 2008.

Neiman, Susan. *Evil in Modern Thought: An Alternative History of Philosophy*. Princeton University Press, 2015.

Nietzsche, Friedrich. *The Gay Science*. Cambridge University Press, 2001.

Pack, Justin. *Amor Mundi and Overcoming Modern World Alienation*. Lexington Books, 2020.

———. "Arendt's Genealogy of Thinking." *Continental Philosophy Review* 50, no. 2 (June 2016): 151–64.

———. *Meritocracy Mingled with Scripture*. By Common Consent Press, 2024.

———. *Money and Thoughtlessness: A Genealogy and Defense of the Traditional Suspicions of Money and Merchants*. Palgrave Macmillan, 2023.

———. "The Need for a Phenomenology of Academic Activity under Neoliberalism." *Interchange* 51, no. 3 (July 2020): 239–52.

———. *Prehistoric Philosophy: The Neolithic Revolution, the Indigenous Critique, and the Myths of Civilization*. Bloomsbury Press, 2026.

Pitkin, Hannah Fenichel. *The Attack of the Blob: Hannah Arendt's Concept of the Social.* University of Chicago Press, 1998.

Plato. *Apology of Socrates.* Translated by Benjamin Jowett. Oxford University Press, 2012.

Polanyi, Karl. *The Great Transformation: The Political and Economic Origins of Our Time.* Beacon Press, 2001.

Porter, Theodore M. *Trust in Numbers: The Pursuit of Objectivity in Science and Public Life.* Princeton University Press, 1996.

Princeton University Press. "On Bullshit Part 1." YouTube. September 18, 2007. Accessed October 10, 2025. https://www.youtube.com/watch?v=W1RO93OS0Sk.

Raisinghani, Vishesh. "'I made millions for doing nothing!': Vanilla Ice built a real estate empire and is reportedly worth $20M now." Yahoo Finance. June 16, 2024. Accessed January 1, 2025. https://finance.yahoo.com/news/made-millions-doing-nothing-vanilla-102000350.html.

Ruddick, Sara. *Maternal Thinking: Towards a Politics of Peace.* Beacon Press, 1995.

Sahlins, Marshall. *The New Science of the Enchanted Universe: An Anthropology of Most of Humanity.* Princeton University Press, 2022.

———. *Stone Age Economics.* Aldine, 1994.

Sandel, Michael J. *The Tyranny of Merit: What's Become of the Common Good?* Farrar, Straus and Giroux, 2020.

Scott, James C. *Against the Grain: A Deep History of the Earliest States.* Yale University Press. 2017.

———. *The Art of Not Being Governed: An Anarchist History of Upland Southeast Asia.* Yale University Press, 2010.

Seneca, Lucius Annaeus. *Letters on Ethics: To Lucilius.* University of Chicago Press, 2020.

Suzman, James. *Affluence Without Abundance: What We Can Learn from the World's Most Successful Civilisation.* Bloomsbury, 2019.

———. "When a 200,000-Year-Old Culture Encountered the Modern Economy." The Atlantic. July 24, 2017. Accessed December 23, 2024. https://www.theatlantic.com/business/archive/2017/07/hunter-gatherers-modern-economy/534522/.

The8431123, "David Mitchell - Customer Service Rant." Youtube. February 13, 2013. Accessed October 17, 2025. https://youtu.be/_LiDTKEF1ek.

Van de Riet, Emily. "Former Teacher Said She Has Made Nearly $1 Million from Onlyfans in Less Than 6 Months." WSFA 12. November 6, 2023. Accessed December 27, 2024. https://www.wsfa.com/2023/11/06/former-teacher-said-she-has-made-nearly-1-million-onlyfans-less-than-6-months/.

Wildcat, Daniel. *On Indigenuity: Learning the Lessons of Mother Earth.* Fulcrum Publishing, 2023.

Williams, Zoe. "Totalitarianism in the Age of Trump: Lessons from Hannah Arendt." The Guardian. February 1, 2017. Accessed July 26, 2020. www.theguardian.com/us-news/2017/feb/01/totalitarianism-in-age-donald-trump-lessons-from-hannah-arendt-protests.

Woods, Vanessa. *Bonobo Handshake: A Memoir of Love and Adventure in the Congo*. Penguin Publishing, 2011.

Yunkaporta, Tyson. *Sand Talk: How Indigenous Thinking Can Save the World.* HarperCollins, 2020.

Index

Also available from

GREG KOFFORD BOOKS

Common Ground—Different Opinions:
Latter-day Saints and Contemporary Issues

Edited by Justin F. White
and James E. Faulconer

Paperback, ISBN: 978-1-58958-573-7

There are many hotly debated issues about which many people disagree, and where common ground is hard to find. From evolution to environmentalism, war and peace to political partisanship, stem cell research to same-sex marriage, how we think about controversial issues affects how we interact as Latter-day Saints.

In this volume various Latter-day Saint authors address these and other issues from differing points of view. Though they differ on these tough questions, they have all found common ground in the gospel of Jesus Christ and the latter-day restoration. Their insights offer diverse points of view while demonstrating we can still love those with whom we disagree.

Praise for *Common Ground—Different Opinions*:

"[This book] provide models of faithful and diverse Latter-day Saints who remain united in the body of Christ. This collection clearly demonstrates that a variety of perspectives on a number of sensitive issues do in fact exist in the Church. . . . [T]he collection is successful in any case where it manages to give readers pause with regard to an issue they've been fond of debating, or convinces them to approach such conversations with greater charity and much more patience. It served as just such a reminder and encouragement to me, and for that reason above all, I recommend this book." — Blair Hodges, Maxwell Institute

The Liberal Soul: Applying the Gospel of Jesus Christ in Politics

Richard Davis

Paperback, ISBN: 978-1-58958-583-6

The Liberal Soul offers something lacking in LDS culture. That is the presentation of a different way for Latter-day Saints to examine the question of how to be faithful disciples of Christ and good citizens. It shows public policy decision-making regarding government role as the manifestation of the "liberal soul" rather than as the libertarianism advocated by past Mormon speakers and writers such as Ezra Taft Benson, Cleon Skousen, or Vern Andersen. It also takes a different approach from the less radical but still traditional economic conservative attitudes of well-known politicians such as Orrin Hatch or Mitt Romney.

Davis suggests that a Latter-day Saint can approach economic policy, war, the environment, and social issues with the perspective that society is basically good and not evil, tolerance and forbearance are desirable qualities instead of bad ones, and that government can and does play a positive role as a vehicle of society in improving the lives of citizens. He describes how Latter-day Saints can apply the Gospel of Jesus Christ to our roles at each of these three levels—individual, group, and society—rather than assuming the societal level violates the principles of the Gospel. The result is that Latter-day Saints can help bring about a Zion society—one where all benefit, the most vulnerable are aided and not ignored, inclusion is the rule and not the exception, and suspicion and fear are replaced by love and acceptance.

Praise for *The Liberal Soul*:

"Davis provides a thoughtful exploration into the principles of generosity, equality, and Christian discipleship and their important relationship to democratic government. This book clearly explains the strong connection between liberalism and Mormonism. I would recommend it to anyone who has ever asked me, 'How can you be a Democrat and a Mormon?'"

— U.S. Senate Majority Leader Harry Reid

The End of the World, Plan B: A Guide for the Future

Charles Shirō Inouye

Paperback, ISBN: 978-1-58958-755-7

Praise for *End of the World, Plan B*:

"Mormonism needs Inouye's voice. We need, in general, voices that are a bit less Ayn Rand and a bit more Siddhartha Gautama. Inouye reminds us that justice is not enough and that obedience is not the currency of salvation. He urges us to recognize the limits of the law, to see that, severed from a willingness to compassionately suffer with the world's imperfection and evanescence, our righteous hunger for balancing life's books will destroy us all."

— Adam S. Miller, author of *Rube Goldberg Machines: Essays in Mormon Theology* and *Letters to a Young Mormon*

"Drawing on Christian, Buddhist, Daoist, and other modes of thought, Charles Inouye shows how an attitude of hope can arise from a narrative of doom. The End of the World, Plan B is not simply a rethinking of the end of our world, but is a meditation on the possibility of compassionate self-transformation. In a world that looks to the just punishment of the wicked, Inouye shows how sorrow, which comes from the demands of justice, can create peace, forgiveness, and love."

— Michael D.K. Ing, Assistant Professor, Department of Religious Studies, Indiana University

"For years I've hoped to see a book that related Mormonism to the great spiritual traditions beyond Christianity and Judaism. Charles Inouye has done this in one of the best Mormon devotional books I've ever read. His Mormon reading of the fourfold path of the Bodhisattva offers a beautiful eschatology of the end/purpose of the world as the revelation of compassion. I hope the book is read widely."

— James M. McLachlan, co-editor of *Discourses in Mormon Theology: Philosophical and Theological Possibilities*

Whom Say Ye That I Am? Lessons from the Jesus of Nazareth

James W. McConkie
and Judith E. McConkie

Paperback, ISBN: 978-1-58958-707-6

"This book is the most important Jesus study to date written by believing Mormons for an LDS audience. It opens the door for Mormons to come to know a Jesus most readers will know little about—the Jesus of history." —David Bokovoy, author of *Authoring the Old Testament: Genesis–Deuteronomy*

"Meticulously documented and researched, the authors have crafted an insightful and enlightening book that allows Jesus to speak by providing both wisdom and council. The McConkies masterfully weave in sources from the Gospels, ancient and modern scholars, along with Christian and non-Christian religious leaders." — *Deseret News*

The story of Jesus is frequently limited to the telling of the babe of Bethlehem who would die on the cross and three days later triumphantly exit his tomb in resurrected glory. Frequently skimmed over or left aside is the story of the Jesus of Nazareth who confronted systemic injustice, angered those in power, risked his life for the oppressed and suffering, and worked to preach and establish the Kingdom of God—all of which would lead to his execution on Calvary.

In this insightful and moving volume, authors James and Judith McConkie turn to the latest scholarship on the historical and cultural background of Jesus to discover lessons on what we can learn from his exemplary life. Whether it be his intimate interactions with the sick, the poor, women, and the outcast, or his public confrontations with oppressive religious, political, and economic institutions, Jesus of Nazareth—the son of a carpenter, Messiah, and Son of God—exemplified the way, the truth, and the life that we must follow to bring about the Kingdom of Heaven.

For Zion: A Mormon Theology of Hope

Joseph M. Spencer

Paperback, ISBN: 978-1-58958-568-3

What is hope? What is Zion? And what does it mean to hope for Zion? In this insightful book, Joseph Spencer explores these questions through the scriptures of two continents separated by nearly two millennia. In the first half, Spencer engages in a rich study of Paul's letter to the Roman to better understand how the apostle understood hope and what it means to have it. In the second half of the book, Spencer jumps to the early years of the Restoration and the various revelations on consecration to understand how Latter-day Saints are expected to strive for Zion. Between these halves is an interlude examining the hoped-for Zion that both thrived in the Book of Mormon and was hoped to be established again.

Praise for *For Zion*:

"Joseph Spencer is one of the most astute readers of sacred texts working in Mormon Studies. Blending theological savvy, historical grounding, and sensitive readings of scripture, he has produced an original and compelling case for consecration and the life of discipleship." — Terryl Givens, author, *Wrestling the Angel: The Foundations of Mormon Thought*

"*For Zion: A Mormon Theology of Hope* is more than a theological reflection. It also consists of able textual exegesis, historical contextualization, and philosophic exploration. Spencer's careful readings of Paul's focus on hope in Romans and on Joseph Smith's development of consecration in his early revelations, linking them as he does with the Book of Mormon, have provided an intriguing, intertextual avenue for understanding what true stewardship should be for us—now and in the future. As such he has set a new benchmark for solid, innovative Latter-day Saint scholarship that is at once provocative and challenging." — Eric D. Huntsman, author, *The Miracles of Jesus*

Imagining and Reimagining the Restoration

Robert A. Rees

Paperback, ISBN: 978-1-58958-828-8

In *Imagining and Reimagining the Restoration,* Robert A. Rees embarks on an imaginative and profound exploration of Latter-day Saint theology and culture. Through essays, poems, and midrashic interpretations, Rees sheds new light on foundational doctrines, the roles of prophetic imagination, and the divine narratives within the Restoration. He reexamines figures like Joseph Smith and Heavenly Mother, urging readers to embrace a creative and expansive faith perspective that transcends mere tradition.

This captivating work brings readers into a visionary discourse that emphasizes the power of imagination as a spiritual gift. With poetic interludes and scholarly insight, this volume is a transformative invitation to both imagine and reimagine faith, theology, and cultural belonging.

Praise for *Imagining and Reimagining the Restoration*:

"This is a beautiful book, a work of art. Enjoining us to imagine the gospel more deeply, it offers reflections on Christ, Mary, the First Vision, Heavenly Mother, and much else. Robert Rees wants to make us all gospel poets. He also seeks to make us religious critics. He gives his candid views of a broken church in need of mending, commenting on race, women's rights, sexual orientation, and earth stewardship with an imagination turned critical but still filled with warmth and good will. In the end, he invites us to imagine a kindly, loving church blessed with modern sensibilities." — Richard Lyman Bushman, author of *Joseph Smith: Rough Stone Rolling*

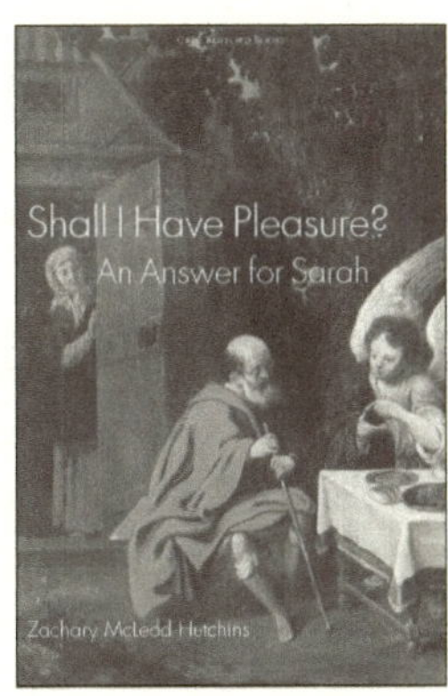

Shall I Have Pleasure?
An Answer for Sarah

Zachary McLeod Hutchins

Paperback, ISBN: 978-1-58958-819-6

Shall I Have Pleasure? An Answer for Sarah explores the complex relationship between faith, desire, and the pursuit of joy through a spiritual and philosophical lens. Drawing from religious narratives, scriptural analysis, and theological insights, the book delves into how pleasure is perceived within Christian traditions, particularly among members of The Church of Jesus Christ of Latter-day Saints. Through reflective anecdotes, historical context, and doctrinal interpretations, the author challenges the tension between spiritual duty and sensory enjoyment, encouraging readers to reconcile divine purpose with the pursuit of happiness.

Rooted in scripture and enriched by personal storytelling, this thought-provoking work invites readers to reconsider long-held beliefs about pleasure and self-denial. By examining biblical stories like Sarah's incredulous laughter at the promise of joy in old age, as well as Christ's compassionate acceptance of human love and generosity, the book offers a fresh perspective on living a life of spiritual fulfillment that embraces joy as an essential part of divine intent. Through this lens, *Shall I Have Pleasure?* becomes a call to rediscover pleasure as a God-given gift intertwined with human purpose and eternal potential.

Praise for *Shall I Have Pleasure?*:

"'Men are, that they might have joy.' But many Latter-day Saints are ambivalent towards—or even skeptical of— the role of pleasure in the joy God wants for us. In *Shall I Have Pleasure?* Zachary Hutchins responds to this confusion with a beautiful and profound affirmation of the divine goodness and gift of pleasure. He invites readers to see pleasure not as a temptation to avoid but an essential and cherished part of our embodied life." — Zachary Davis, Executive Director of Faith Matters and Editor of *Wayfare Magazine*

And There Was No Poor Among Them: Liberation, Salvation, and the Meaning of the Restoration

Ryan D. Ward

Paperback, ISBN: 978-1-58958-787-8

While The Church of Jesus Christ of Latter-day Saints has expanded many fundamental Christian doctrines, salvation is still understood as pertaining exclusively to the next life. How should we understand salvation and what does the timing of the Restoration reveal about God's vision of salvation for a suffering world?

To answer these questions, author Ryan Ward traces the theological evolution of salvation from the liberation of Israel from oppression to the Western Christian development of salvation as an individualistic, transactional atonement. This evolution corresponded with the shift of Christianity from a covenant community to an official state religion aligned with imperial power structures. Ward also explores the economic and social movements in the centuries leading up to the Industrial Revolution, which solidified the power of propertied elites at the expense of the poor, plundered entire continents, and killed millions.

Synthesizing these theological and historical threads, *And There Was No Poor Among Them: Liberation, Salvation, and the Meaning of the Restoration* asserts that the Restoration is God's explicit rejection of social and economic systems and ideologies that have led to the globalization of misery. Instead, Ward shows how the Restoration and the gospel of Christ is an invitation to a participatory salvation realized in Zion communities where "there are no poor among us."

Praise for *And There Was No Poor Among Them*:

"This a profound and profoundly important book, one of the most compelling in the history of modern Mormonism. . . . If I had the power, I would make *And There Was No Poor Among Them* required reading of every local, regional, and general leader of the Church." — Robert A. Rees, co-founder and vice-president of the Bountiful Children's Foundation

www.ingramcontent.com/pod-product-compliance
Lightning Source LLC
LaVergne TN
LVHW051024080826
845145LV00009B/2785

* 9 7 8 1 5 8 9 5 8 8 2 3 3 *